At a time when religious liberty is  the church needs prophetic voice *tion* she exposes the liberal politi Christian packaging and sold to evangelical Left's cunning distortion of scripture is bad for the body of Christ—and for the nation as a whole. But all is not lost. Vicari not only reveals the evangelical Left's tactics, she also explains how the church can steer Millennials back toward the truth. This is a critical message for the church to read and apply. I highly recommend it.

—TODD STARNES
Host, *Fox News & Commentary*
Author, *God Less America*

Distortion targets one of the prime dangers to the American church: professing Christians who use biblical language to advance very liberal political agenda. Their deception, couched in the misuse of Scripture, is a threat to the spiritual vitality of the church in our time. An important new voice among evangelical millennials, Chelsen Vicari demonstrates how the efforts of the "Christian Left" have deceived many—and why they need to be exposed and rejected by faithful Christians. Her book is thorough, readable, and timely. I hope it has a wide readership, and its truths even wider application.

—TONY PERKINS
President, Family Research Council

Chelsen Vicari is a rising star for evangelicals in America. She knows the strengths and weaknesses of Christian faith and practice among her own Millennials. And she has the boldness to challenge the often boring and wrong conventional wisdom. Persons of all ages and beliefs will profit from and enjoy reading her unique analysis.

—MARK TOOLEY
President, Institute on Religion and Democracy

While reading Chelsen Vicari's *Distortion*, words such as *bracing*, *formidable*, and *insightful* kept popping into my mind. Ms. Vicari has done a great service for her millennial generation as well as for all of her fellow Americans of faith by exposing the inconsistencies and inadequacies of many of the trendy movements among millennial Christians. She is fearless in taking on the "emergent" movement as well as exposing the "social justice façade" and the politically correct feminism that too often permeate the evangelical Left.

Every evangelical Christian needs to read this book. It will illuminate, educate, and liberate all who dare engage its arguments with an open mind.

—Dr. Richard Land
President, Southern Evangelical Seminary
Charlotte, NC

A much-needed book by a Millennial about why so many of her generation have given up on evangelical Christianity. Wisdom beyond her years, keen insight, research that is both deep and wide, and a grasp of the culture make this book must-reading for anyone who wants to know how to reach today's generation for Christ and His kingdom.

—Janice Shaw Crouse, PhD
Author, *Children at Risk* and *Marriage Matters*

Chelsen Vicari is a rare voice in the Christian world today. She's bold, careful, and refuses to cower. In this new volume she goes after the shibboleths and sacred cows of the Christian Left. In flowing prose she exposes the subtleties that lead astray and the deviations that tear historic, biblical Christianity asunder. She doesn't hold back. Some will disagree with her conclusions, but they can't deny her passion.

—Andrew Walker
Director of policy studies, Southern Baptist Convention's
Ethics & Religious Liberty Commission

Vicari's weapon is the mighty pen, and her book exposes the Left while advocating for the sanctity of human life, the traditional family, and religious liberty.

—Eric Patterson, PhD
Dean, Robertson School of Government
Regent University

Since the snake in the garden, tempters have wriggled into communities of God's followers to whisper and lure people away. Young evangelicals are the latest target for appealing challenges to their faith. Chelsen Vicari reveals the attractive arguments for the traps they are, and provides truth straight from God's Word as the antidote.

—Wendy Wright
Pro-life and pro-family advocate, former president of Concerned
Women for America, vice president of C-FAM

DISTORTION

CHELSEN VICARI

Most CHARISMA HOUSE BOOK GROUP products are available at special quantity discounts for bulk purchase for sales promotions, premiums, fund-raising, and educational needs. For details, write Charisma House Book Group, 600 Rinehart Road, Lake Mary, Florida 32746, or telephone (407) 333-0600.

DISTORTION by Chelsen Vicari
Published by FrontLine
Charisma Media/Charisma House Book Group
600 Rinehart Road
Lake Mary, Florida 32746
www.charismahouse.com

This book or parts thereof may not be reproduced in any form, stored in a retrieval system, or transmitted in any form by any means—electronic, mechanical, photocopy, recording, or otherwise—without prior written permission of the publisher, except as provided by United States of America copyright law.

Unless otherwise noted, all Scripture quotations are from the Holy Bible, English Standard Version. Copyright © 2001 by Crossway Bibles, a division of Good News Publishers. Used by permission.

Scripture quotations marked NAS are from the New American Standard Bible, copyright © 1960, 1962, 1963, 1968, 1971, 1972, 1973, 1975, 1977, 1995 by The Lockman Foundation. Used by permission. (www.Lockman.org)

Scripture quotations marked NIV are taken from the Holy Bible, New International Version®, NIV®. Copyright © 1973, 1978, 1984, 2011 by Biblica, Inc.™ Used by permission of Zondervan. All rights reserved worldwide. www.zondervan.com The "NIV" and "New International Version" are trademarks registered in the United States Patent and Trademark Office by Biblica, Inc.™

Scripture quotations marked NKJV are taken from the New King James Version®. Copyright © 1982 by Thomas Nelson. Used by permission. All rights reserved.

Scripture quotations marked NLT are from the Holy Bible, New Living Translation, copyright © 1996, 2004, 2007. Used by permission of Tyndale House Publishers, Inc., Wheaton, IL 60189. All rights reserved.

Copyright © 2014 by Chelsen Vicari
All rights reserved

Cover design by Justin Evans

Visit the author's website at www.theird.org/evangelical/.

Library of Congress Cataloging-in-Publication Data:
Vicari, Chelsen.
  Distortion / by Chelsen Vicari. -- First edition.
     pages cm
  Includes bibliographical references.
  ISBN 978-1-62998-020-1 (trade paper) -- ISBN 978-1-62998-021-8 (e-book)
  1. Liberalism (Religion) 2. Liberalism (Religion)--United States. 3. United States--Church history--20th century. 4. United States--Church history--21st century. I. Title.
  BR1617.V53 2014
  277.3'083--dc23

                              2014024867

First edition

14 15 16 17 18 — 9 8 7 6 5 4 3 2 1
Printed in the United States of America

Lovingly dedicated to Mom and Dad,
cherished spiritual mentors and prayer warriors,
who willingly share God's truth in love.

CONTENTS

INTRODUCTION

"IGNORE THE PHONE CALL. GET BACK TO WRITING." THIS IS what I was thinking as I was working late in my office in downtown Washington DC on a rainy December evening.

I had dealt with a myriad of emotional blows at work that day, and I was weary. I didn't think I had any strength left to chitchat with what I assumed would be a curious reader of my blog. I felt as though my world, which revolved around young evangelicals, was crumbling, and no one my age, or older for that matter, seemed to care. Faking cheeriness was just not an option.

I had spent the entire day trying to scrimp together enough funds to keep alive the Institute for Religion and Democracy's (IRD) new ministry, Evangelical Action. I reached out to everyone I thought might be willing to financially and prayerfully support our unique ministry seeking to revive the social witness of America's young evangelicals. Sadly I received a lot of "I'll pray about its" and a few outright noes, and I was feeling pretty discouraged.

On the job as director of Evangelical Action for only two months at that time, I had been hired to engage and empower young evangelicals. I knew they had been buying into distorted religious teachings, but the more I probed to understand their thinking and beliefs, the more I realized I needed to brush up on my knowledge of various New Age and humanist philosophies, because they were quietly influencing young Christians' beliefs. As I scoured the Internet for something that would help me wrap my brain around the concept of existentialism, I came across an article that left me speechless.

It was titled "Not Believing Anything." In it a twenty-six-year-old man explained how he came to abandon God and embrace a mystical pursuit of greater purpose. When I glanced at the author's name, a wave of nausea washed over me as I recognized the byline. The article was written by one of my close childhood friends. He and I grew up in the same Assemblies of God church. Our parents attended the same small group and often swapped playdates. In Sunday school this boy knew every Bible quiz answer. I mean, this was the kid I wanted to beat when it came time for sword drills in children's church. He always won. I knew him to love Jesus unlike any other kid in my church social circle. Yet now I was reading about how he decided to let go of God in exchange for a belief system built on nothingness.

There in black and white was yet another example of a young evangelical who had been wooed away from authentic faith. There was yet another reminder of the great need for a ministry that would help young Christians discover the truth before they drifted off into error or unbelief. I wanted to see my generation become countercultural for Christ. And yet, where was the support for such an effort? Where was the sense of urgency for the future of evangelicalism?

I was sitting at my desk exasperated and disheartened when the phone rang. I was in no mood to pick up. Thank God I answered anyway.

"Praise God, I got through!" cracked the jolly voice. "I want to help."

The man was a self-described Pentecostal Baptist who had been on IRD's mailing list for years. "I'm excited!" he said. "I can see the impact you're trying to make. I too am deeply concerned for the direction of evangelicals."

The jolly voice regretted that he could not offer me financial support because he was on a fixed income. But the encouragement he gave was priceless. The man whom I'll call Allen had served as an evangelist for many years, and he knew firsthand the challenges—financial, emotional, and spiritual—of calling his generation to return to the traditional teachings of Scripture.

Allen was now a concerned parent. His daughter was a godly young woman who worked as a nurse in the children's unit of a major hospital. Passionately pro-life, she struggled daily with medical decisions that diminished the sanctity of life. Despite being ridiculed, Allen explained, his daughter refused to compromise God's instruction to defend innocent life.

"I didn't know others existed who were young and bold for Christ," he said. "And then I got your ministry letter."

"Funny," I replied. "I was starting to think the same thing about your generation. Thank God you called!"

During that phone call, undoubtedly orchestrated by the good Lord, I felt renewed hope for my generation. I felt relief and thankfulness that there exist concerned parents, grandparents, youth ministers, Sunday school teachers, and pastors who recognize America's spiritual and moral decline and desperately want to find a solution.

America's "grown-ups," who have the ability to influence and pray for young Christians, must not declare defeat and give up on us. Instead, they must start understanding and confronting the false, partisan teachings influencing the next generation of evangelicals and take back America's Christian culture.

So when I thought about writing a book on how we prevent the next generation of evangelicals from drifting away from authentic Christianity and the principles that have made America great, Allen's phone call came to mind. I knew the most important thing I could do was help concerned family members, teachers, and ministry leaders understand how my generation is being deceived and how they can help get America's moral majority back on track.

Through this book it is my hope that mentors will be armed

with Scripture, historic Christian teaching, and social science that specifically addresses the challenges—homosexuality, feminism, and religious persecution, to name a few—confronting Christians in a culture increasingly hostile to truth in love.

Above all, this book will be a twenty-first-century reminder that just as Christ was deemed offensive for standing for truth, so will His followers. But the good news is that Christ never leaves us standing alone.

Allen reminded me of this truth just before we ended the call. "Chelsen," he said, "it is worth the battle."

It is time for the "adults in the room" to take a stand once again in the culture wars, this time for the sake of America's young evangelicals. Through your example your generation can teach my Millennial generation to keep praying, keep acting, keep discerning truth, keep upholding Scripture as the authority, and keep fighting on the battleground where Christianity and public policy collide.

Dear readers, it is worth the battle.

—Chelsen Vicari

PART ONE:
THE CRISIS

> *Therefore take up the whole armor of God, that you may be able to withstand in the evil day, and having done all, to stand.*
>
> — EPHESIANS 6:13–14, NKJV

Chapter 1

FACING THE PROBLEM

> *If we really want a Christian society*
> *we must teach Christianity.*[1]
> DOROTHY SAYERS

PEEK BEHIND THE CURTAIN OF SOME "HIP" OR "PROGRES-
sive" evangelical churches, past the savvy technology and
secular music, and you will find more than just a contemporary worship service. You'll find faith leaders encouraging young
evangelicals to trade in their Christian convictions for a gospel
filled with compromise. They're slowly attempting to give evangelicalism an "update"—and the change is not for the good.

It's painful for me to admit, but we can no longer rest carefree
in our evangelical identity—because it is changing. No doubt you
have seen the headlines declaring that evangelicalism is doomed
because evangelical kids are leaving the faith. It is no secret that
there is an expanding gulf between traditional Christian teachings and contemporary moral values. But the sad truth is that
the ideological gulf between America's evangelical grown-ups
and their kids, aka the "Millennials," seems to be widening too.

Somehow the blame for this chasm is being heaped on

traditional churches, or those that espouse a classic Christian orthodoxy. They are accused of having too many rules and being homophobic and bigoted. Yes, we've heard those false claims from popular culture in its desperate attempt to keep Christianity imprisoned within the sanctuary walls. But now popular culture is being aided by Christ-professing bedfellows whose message to "coexist," "tolerate," and "keep out of it" is more marketable to the rising generation of evangelicals.

The seasoned Christian soldiers are noticing these distortions of the gospel (which, by the way, has always been countercultural). But for young evangelicals the spiritual haze is harder to wade through. Desperate for acceptance in a fallen world, many young evangelicals (and some older ones) choose not to take Christ out of the chapel, and so they are unwittingly killing the church's public witness. In this uphill cultural battle, mired by scare tactics and fear, three types of evangelical Christians are emerging:

- **Couch-potato Christians:** These Christians adapt to the culture by staying silent on the tough culture and faith discussions. Typically this group will downplay God's absolute truths by promoting the illusion that neutrality was Jesus's preferred method of evangelism.

- **Cafeteria-style Christians:** This group picks and chooses which Scripture passages to live by, opting for the ones that best seem to jive with culture. Typically they focus solely on the "nice" parts of the gospel while simultaneously and intentionally minimizing sin, hell, repentance, and transformation.

- **Convictional Christians:** In the face of the culture's harsh admonitions, these evangelicals refuse

to be silent. Mimicking Jesus, they compassion-
ately talk about love and grace while also sharing
with their neighbors the need to recognize and
turn from sin.

I know about these three types of Christians because at one time or another I have fallen into each of these three categories. My parents will tell you that even though I was raised in church, I morphed into a full-fledged feminist, told my parents they were ignorant for not endorsing homosexuality, and bought into the distorted social justice rhetoric that confuses caring for the poor with advancing socialist or big government systems and demonizing the United States for its free market system.

I'm not ashamed to share my story for two reasons. First, I pray that it will help you better understand the cultural challenges stifling the evangelical community's social and political witness. Second, and most important, my experiences and those of my fellow bold evangelicals are a testimony of God's awesome, transforming power at work in classrooms, pews, and the nation.

Being countercultural for Christ isn't easy. Trust me, I've felt awkward and uncomfortable talking about politics and religion in big groups too. But it's not a choice we have. What does the Great Commission say? Jesus commanded us to go, "teaching them to obey everything I have commanded you" (Matt. 28:20, NIV). Jesus said for us to share "everything," not just what is convenient.

If the church—and by that I mean Christ-professing parents, teachers, mentors, pastors, and friends, all entrusted with equipping young disciples in biblical knowledge—does not talk about the tough moral issues and examine what the Bible says at home, in class, and around church, then I can promise you the world will.

Kissing Evangelicalism Good-Bye?

I see so many parents (including my own at one time) scratching their heads trying to figure out where they went wrong with young evangelicals. Following the instructions of Proverbs 22:6—"Train up a child in the way he should go, and when he is old he will not depart from it" (NKJV)—many evangelical parents took their children to church and prayed with them every night before bed. Yet the values those children now hold dear do not reflect the traditional teachings of Jesus.

To be perfectly clear, I want to let you know upfront that this book isn't a parenting how-to guide that, if followed, will lead your loved ones to salvation. Salvation is easily attainable but found only through Jesus Christ. Instead, what I can offer you is a glimpse into the world of a twentysomething who sees thousands of young evangelicals being spiritually and emotionally targeted on Christian university campuses, in college ministries, and at churches nationwide by a growing liberal movement cloaked in Christianity. Within these evangelical institutions, and even in some sanctuaries, truth has been made relative. Scripture verses that reference anything considered offensive are skipped over, and God's supremacy is diminished in order to market the church to as wide an audience as possible.

Evidence for this moral and spiritual decline is staring us straight in the eye. Research tells us that evangelicals are drifting further away from the orthodox truths their parents and grandparents held dear. Baptists, the country's largest Protestant group, are departing from their religious traditions faster than other evangelicals. According to a 2008 Pew Research study, of all the Protestant groups, Baptists had the largest percentage of children who chose not to affiliate with them as adults, experiencing a net change of 3.7 percent.[2] The only other church tradition with a greater loss was the Catholic Church with a loss of 7.5 percent.[3]

In addition, LifeWay Research found the number of members affiliated with the Southern Baptist Convention (SBC) declined by more than one hundred thousand in one year.[4] A comparison between 1980 and 2005 found that the number of yearly young adult baptisms decreased by forty thousand people.[5]

It gets worse. During his remarks to the SBC's 2001 Executive Committee, T. C. Pinckney, the convention's vice president at the time, made an astonishing admission. He said research revealed that approximately 70 percent of youth were leaving the church within two years of their high school graduations.[6] Many young Baptists have also admitted that they are starting to view the church as irrelevant to their lives.[7]

Our churches have rarely—if ever—faced the exodus we are seeing today. This will have a direct effect on the spiritual and moral values that will shape the nation in the coming years. That is why it is urgent that concerned Christians start acting now before the situation gets worse.

Conviction, Corruption, and Bad Theology

Faith and culture will continue to collide in America. However, it is the nation's faith convictions that will ultimately determine the direction of not only culture but also the economy and government. The culture wars, the growth of family, the success of missions, the prosperity of our great nation—the future rests on Millennial evangelicals' worldview. And that is cause for concern, because something has gone terribly wrong with young evangelicals' theology.

The Millennial generation's susceptibility to "feel-good" doctrine is playing a big part in America's moral decline. Millennials' religious practices depend largely on how the actions make us and others *feel*, whether the activities are biblical or not. For example, we only attend churches that leave us feeling good about our lifestyle choices, even if those choices conflict with

God's clear commandments. We dismiss old hymns that focus on God's transforming salvation, love, and mercy and opt for "Jesus is your boyfriend" songs. Or we contribute to nonprofits that exploit and misuse terms such as *justice, oppressed,* and *inequality* because tweaking the language makes us feel more neutral, less confrontational.

The truth is that following Christ is not merely about endorsing grace and love, but it also about obeying a set of commandments established by our Creator. That is why Jesus said: "Anyone who loves me will obey my teaching. My Father will love them, and we will come to them and make our home with them" (John 14:23, NIV).

Popular culture often gets "truth" wrong, especially when it comes to religion. Even in the twenty-first century the apostle John's warning still applies: "For many deceivers have gone out into the world who do not confess Jesus Christ as coming in the flesh. This is a deceiver and an antichrist. Look to yourselves, that we do not lose those things we worked for, but that we may receive a full reward" (2 John 7–8, NKJV).

Popular liberal evangelical writers and preachers tell young evangelicals that if they accept abortion and same-sex marriage, then the media, academia, and Hollywood will finally accept Christians. Out of fear of being falsely dubbed "intolerant" or "uncompassionate," many young Christians are buying into theological falsehoods. Instead of standing up as a voice for the innocent unborn or marriage as God intended, Millennials are forgoing the authority of Scripture and embracing a couch-potato, cafeteria-style Christianity all in the name of tolerance.

This contemporary mind-set is what Dietrich Bonhoeffer, the German theologian whose Christian convictions put him at odds with the Nazis and cost him his life, called "cheap grace." In his book *The Cost of Discipleship* Bonhoeffer wrote:

> Cheap grace is the preaching of forgiveness without requiring repentance, baptism without church discipline, Communion without confession, absolution without personal confession. Cheap grace is grace without discipleship, grace without the cross, grace without Jesus Christ, living and incarnate.[8]

Waving the white flag of defeat in the culture wars is not an option for today's evangelicals because to do so would be to give up on the next generation's walk with Christ. Right now cheap-grace theology is proliferating around evangelical Bible colleges, seminaries, and Christian ministries and dictating young people's convictions. It is important for culture-warrior Christians to speak out, as Bonhoeffer did, against the popular trends and act as role models for the next generation.

What Went Wrong?

It is not that Millennial evangelicals were not taken to church by their parents or taught about Jesus in Sunday school. It is that their training has been hijacked by ineffective, inaccurate, and, sometimes, intentionally distorted doctrine.

An army of evangelicals is being raised up on Christian campuses, and we pray that their theology remains founded on the authority of God's Word and not the lips of nice-sounding strangers. For those young evangelicals who attend public undergraduate schools as I did, well, we just have to pray that much more fervently that they do not walk away from their faith.

As constant and pervasive as the attacks on Christianity are at public universities, it is important to remember that Millennials' worldviews do not start taking shape after they move out of their parents' houses and into their dorm rooms. Their understanding of Jesus's teachings and cultural convictions begin to form while they are still at home and under the influence of their local church.

During the summer of 2012 I was sitting in the youth minister's office at my local church. The middle-school class was in need of an additional Sunday school teacher, and I was up for the job. The youth minister and I talked about my personal testimony, my family's beliefs, and my criminal record. (Rest assured, parents, I don't have one!) Then suddenly the youth minister's expression darkened, and his tone turned very serious when he confessed the biggest challenge he was facing. He told me, "I'm watching these kids be raised in church. They memorize Scripture. They know who Jesus is and what He taught. But then they move away to college and let go of those teachings. They go wild. We have to figure out what is happening." The ministry director was right, and once I started teaching Sunday school, I quickly figured out why he was seeing this trend.

What I hope and pray evangelical parents and leaders come to realize is that the church has been too trusting. In our jam-packed lifestyles, parents have treated Sunday school as they do softball or ballet class—drop off the kids for an hour then pick them up and hope they learned something. But Christian teaching once a week by leaders and volunteers, some of whom do not uphold traditional Christian teaching, is not enough to equip young evangelicals.

Early on in my Sunday school teaching days, my co-teacher and I followed the curriculum pretty narrowly, the exception being that my co-teacher had an outstanding knowledge of biblical history that he imparted to the kids. Me? As a pro-family, pro-life advocate, I could have taken the full hour to unload about the pro-abortion movement's racist origins or the emotional impact of being raised by gay parents.

Unfortunately, being new to this particular Sunday school class, I held back my outrages with pop culture. We taught all about Jesus's birth, resurrection, and saving grace. Thinking the fluffy kids' ministry curriculum covered all of the necessary bases,

I felt confident these kids had a firm grasp on their Christian worldview. Boy, was I wrong!

One day my co-teacher and I decided to play "True or False." We casually went down a list of worldview questions with our class, sure that our little evangelicals would nail every question correctly.

1. **Number one:** Jesus is God. "True." Great job.

2. **Number two:** Jesus sinned. "False." Bingo!

3. **Number three:** Jesus is one of many ways to heaven. "True." What?!

Shocked is the only way to describe how I felt. Hadn't they been listening to us, or their parents, or their youth pastor? When I asked who taught them that, one girl said, "Coexist." Yes, these young evangelicals had been listening to their Sunday school teachers and their parents, but they had also been listening to their public schoolteachers, non-Christian friends, TV celebrities, and rock stars. It wasn't enough to teach these youngsters the basic tenets of Christianity. Because we never addressed what secular society was teaching them too, they came to accept everything and anything.

Youth ministers, volunteer leaders, and pastors have to start preparing these kids to deal with the very real hostility that faces young evangelicals. In addition to encouraging our kids to memorize Scripture and participate in Christmas plays, we must prepare them from an early age to confront the opposition to their beliefs that will come from inside and outside the church realm. We must teach them by speaking boldly and intelligently to serious, controversial cultural issues. Scripture cuts to the point on this very topic.

But as for you, teach what accords with sound doctrine. Older men are to be sober-minded, dignified, self-
controlled, sound in faith, in love, and in steadfastness.
Older women likewise are to be reverent in behavior, not
slanderers or slaves to much wine. They are to teach what
is good, and so train the young women to love their husbands and children, to be self-controlled, pure, working at
home, kind, and submissive to their own husbands, that
the word of God may not be reviled.

Likewise, urge the younger men to be self-controlled.
Show yourself in all respects to be a model of good works,
and in your teaching show integrity, dignity, and sound
speech that cannot be condemned, so that an opponent
may be put to shame, having nothing evil to say about us.

—TITUS 2:1–8

According to Jon Nielson, the college ministry director at
College Church in Wheaton, Illinois, youth who stay in church
through their college years have been "equipped, not entertained."
Nielson explained, "Christ gives us—teachers—to the church,
not for entertainment, encouragement, examples, or even friendship primarily. He gives us to the church to 'equip' the saints to
do gospel ministry, in order that the church of Christ may be
built up."[9]

If we never talk about abortion in church, how can we expect
the rising evangelical girl to calmly explain the option of adoption to her frightened best friend who just admitted she is pregnant? Do we really expect that fifteen-year-old evangelical boy
to not view pornography if we fail to mention that smut lends to
the capture and rape of sex trafficking victims, or how it simply
is not reality and destroys families?

What will surprise you is how much young evangelicals actually crave honest discussions about abortion, sexuality, sexual
exploitation, feminism, and radical Islam. My friend and

Evangelical Action adviser, Richmond Trotter, has two nonnegotiable topics when addressing youth: creation and life. Having volunteered in church youth ministry since 1996, Richmond is not afraid to have serious discussions about what Scripture says about abortion, evolution, and homosexuality. While apprenticing under Richmond, I watched him tie the planned lesson into discussions about the selflessness of adoption, religious persecution at home and abroad, and radical Islam—all in one hour. Now that is what it means to effectively "raise up a child in the way he should go"!

Most importantly, I vividly remember how engaged the students were. Forget raising hands; the kids just boldly asked the questions on their minds. Or they told us what their friends at school were going through and asked us how the Bible would have them help. These kids were already facing the culture and faith issues Richmond brought up and were desperate for answers but were too afraid to ask—that is, until someone initiated the conversation. Then we couldn't get them to stop talking. It was glorious and one of those life lessons I shall never forget.

Make no mistake: the trend away from biblical truth is not concentrated in the hipster city limits. It is unfolding in the crevices of America's plains, hills, mountains, and swamplands. All across this nation, "old-fashioned" conservative evangelicalism is being traded in for a bright and shiny mediocre Christianity. It is up to you, dear reader, to change the trajectory of faith and culture in America. Memorize and mediate on the words of Ephesians 4:11–12: "And He Himself gave some to be apostles, some prophets, some evangelists, and some pastors and teachers, for the equipping of the saints for the work of ministry, for the edifying of the body of Christ" (NKJV).

If America's evangelicals disengage from the public square and fail to engage the rising generation of Christian leaders, then we risk losing our public voice, then our religious liberty, then liberty altogether.

Is the Religious Right Lifeless?

The last several decades witnessed tremendous evangelical influence in the United States. Leaders such as Billy Graham, Jerry Falwell, Pat Robertson, Tim and Beverly LaHaye, Paige and Dorothy Patterson, James Dobson, and James and Betty Robison made a bold impact on America's families, churches, and government. Now that those few leaders are aging or retiring, or have passed away, there are very few traditional evangelical leaders left holding the torch and even fewer candidates to whom they can pass it.

The *Daily Caller*'s senior contributor, Matt Lewis, has dubbed Millennials the "post-culture war generation" of Christians. Lewis wrote, "I've written a lot lately about how conservatives lost the culture war. Some of my socially conservative friends were upset when I argued that at least part of the reason for this was that 'pro-family' activist groups aren't as effective as fiscally conservative groups."[10] Sadly, what fiscal conservatives like Lewis have not figured out is that the culture wars are not about partisan politics. They never were. Sure, some high-profile figures on both the Right and the Left have highlighted certain social issues to get elected. But the evangelical grassroots' involvement in the culture wars has always been, and will continue to be, grounded in conviction.

Pascal-Emmanuel Gobry, *Forbes* contributor on global strategic issues, agrees that it is not time to write the culture warrior's epitaph yet. He explained:

> You could argue that these people are old and therefore doomed to going away, but again no dice: though opposition to same-sex marriage is very weak among the young, as

many if not more young people are pro-life than the older cohort (and abortion has always been and will remain, for good or ill, the salient issue of the culture war).[11]

Let me just say that hundreds of thousands of pro-life Americans do not take time off work, spend money on travel and lodging, and brave Washington DC's frigid January temperatures to march for a political candidate. Thanks to changing hearts and minds, both old and young demonstrate their convictions against the murder of the innocent by participating in the March for Life—and they will not stop until abortion is finally abolished.

Religious convictions in America are not on the verge of disappearance just yet. There is still hope. In the book *God Is Alive and Well: The Future of Religion in America*, Gallup Inc. editor-in-chief Frank Newport ensures: "Right now, we don't see any signs of an unusual increase in non-Christian religions. Christianity will prevail in the U.S. America will remain very much a Christian nation in the decades ahead, albeit less so than in the past because of an increase in Americans who don't have a religious identity."[12]

Heed the Warning Signs

Evangelicals and culture warriors do not have to look far to discover what happens when Christian denominations give up on their traditional convictions and teachings. All we have to do is look at the example of mainline Protestant denominations—the United Methodists, Episcopalians, Presbyterians, United Church of Christ (UCC), and Lutherans.

Before I go any further, I must make a confession. When I joined the staff of the Institute on Religion and Democracy (IRD), I dismissed mainline denominations such as the United Methodist Church as liberal and thought they were beyond saving. Shame on me for giving up so easily! Thank God I discovered IRD's United Methodist Action (UMAction) ministry, which was established by United Methodist leaders David Jessup and Rev. Edmund Robb to challenge radical leftist leaders, or "revisionists," as they are often called, within their church.

Today UMAction leaders Mark Tooley and John Lomperis have numerous stories of victory in their efforts to bring a renewal of orthodoxy. But UMAction faces an ongoing battle against radical United Methodist leadership, and the quest to limit their damaging impact continues. We evangelicals should take note of ministries such as the IRD's UMAction, Anglican Action, and Religious Persecution and apply similar principles in our own communities.

The similarity between where the mainline Protestants have been and where evangelicals are heading is just plain scary. For many mainline denominations the descent down the slippery slope of compromise started when they embraced the social gospel movement. This cause stressed the need for salvation from poverty, inequality, and oppression over forgiveness of sins through Christ—all in order to accommodate the opinions of secular society.[13] (This sounds familiar, right?) This movement backfired. Almost immediately after adopting the social gospel and forgoing traditional Christian teachings that were deemed offensive and exclusionary, mainline membership began to decline, and congregants no longer affirmed the role of faith in their lives. These denominations didn't know it at the time, but the church needs *all* of the gospel to see lives, cities, and nations transformed.

Since then two mainline denominations have attempted to reverse the decades of membership loss. Between 2001 and 2008 IRD reported that the United Methodist Church spent $47 million on television ads in hopes of igniting congregation growth. In 2004 the wildly secular UCC—a denomination that endorses abortion and same-sex marriage—launched similar television commercial ads. But because the church did not also change its teachings, the campaign was worthless—so ineffective, in fact, that two hundred more congregations actually withdrew their membership from the UCC within one year after the campaign was launched.[14]

The continued decline makes sense to me. Why continue to attend a church that says truth is whatever you make it to be? I mean, why sit under a minister who simply encourages you to determine good and evil on your own? We can do that at home in our pajamas.

Beyond the church walls, radical liberal teachings also have been permeating mainline Protestant seminaries since the beginning of the twentieth century.[15] This also has contributed to mainline churches' plummeting membership. The National Opinion Research Center at the University of Chicago noted that the mainline Protestant churches began their rapid decline because their institutions failed to adequately engage and intellectually stimulate their own youth. Dr. Lewis Andrews, executive director of the Yankee Institute for Public Policy in Hartford, Connecticut, rightly noted, "Only by providing an education that rises to the challenge of secular culture can Protestant denominations ever give large numbers of youngsters the intellectual strength and stamina to be practicing Christians in the modern world."[16]

I am so sorry to say that if you stop and investigate even the most prominent evangelical colleges and seminaries, you will discover that liberal doctrine runs rampant. Some Christian colleges such as Belmont University in Nashville, Tennessee, are endorsing official gay student groups on campus.[17] The traditional Christian doctrine taught within evangelical campuses is, well, not so traditional anymore. Be still, my soul. (We will discuss the decline of Christian colleges further in chapter 5 when we uncover the social justice disguise.)

The takeaway here is the evangelical community can never embrace actions clearly outlined by Scripture as sin. To do so is to sacrifice God's authority, commandments, and blessings for humanity on the grand altar of tolerance. Let this be a lesson for evangelicals to speak out against misleading theology and dangerous compromise. As A. W. Tozer wrote, "We are sent to bless the world, but never are we told to compromise with it."[18]

Renewal groups such as the IRD and the Association for Church Renewal continue to uphold the authoritative Word of God as the standard for faith and ethics for mainline churches and "a culture in confusion." Their work is challenging. Finding support, encouragement, and prayer is extremely difficult. Still they refuse to quit. So too should evangelicals.

In order to safeguard the trajectory of young evangelicals (and, inadvertently, the well-being of our nation), we must take a similar stance. It is imperative that those in a position to influence Millennials have transparent and honest discussions about the culture wars evangelical youth are already engaging. Otherwise they will be silent and accepting in the face of persecution and false doctrine.

The importance of arming the next generation of evangelicals cannot be overstated. If we continue to follow the example of mainline Protestants, evangelicalism will have a gloomy future. We must offer sorely needed leadership, but before we can do that, we need to know exactly *whom* and *what* we are up against.

Chapter 2

WHEN FAITH MEETS CULTURE

> *May He who searches the hearts*
> *of the children of men, prosper*
> *your exertions to secure the*
> *blessings peace and promote the*
> *highest welfare of our country.*[1]
>
> — JOHN QUINCY ADAMS

ELECTION SEASON IS AN EXHAUSTING AND SOMETIMES NAU-
seating time for Americans. Smear campaigns are ever-
popular among politicians and their campaign staff. Now-
adays, lying, cheating, and false accusations appear to be the
norm. Even the most seemingly wholesome candidates sacrifice
their morals on the glitzy road to Washington DC.

I traveled a different route into Washington. Newly graduated
from Regent University in May 2011, I had just taken my first
job inside the pro-family movement with Concerned Women
for America (CWA), the nation's largest public policy women's
institute. The job was administrative. That's a nicer way of con-
fessing that I mostly answered phones. Far from glamorous, my

commute into the city consisted of two bumpy buses and the dingy Metro train. It was miserable. It is still my daily commute.

By October 21, 2011, I was ready to leave Washington and never return. Political fatigue and emotional exhaustion had fully set in. Living in the DC area turned out to be tough for a young conservative evangelical woman. The city was competitive, dangerous, and unaffordable on a shoestring, nonprofit budget. Feeling beaten down, I wanted to move back to my hometown. But God had different expectations.

Sitting behind the CWA reception desk feeling slightly depressed and buckling under the pressures, I wrote a simple prayer in my journal: "God, what am I doing here?" Shortly after I wrote that prayer, the office door opened and Christian historian and author William Federer walked in to lead a lecture. Perhaps sensing my despair, Mr. Federer offered me a complimentary copy of his book *America's God and Country*. Asking for my name, Mr. Federer flipped open the coverlet and wrote four God-inspired words that gave me much-needed hope and direction: *"Chelsen, America needs you!"*

America Needs You

Right now America's young evangelicals need leadership, and we are not getting much from many of our elected representatives. As a result, national leadership and wisdom must start coming from America's pulpits, parents, and perhaps even nonprofit receptionists.

So often I hear evangelical leaders proclaim, "If the government stays out of my business, I'll stay out of its business." These sentiments are understandable. The corruption and constant bickering among politicians get old after a while. But there are serious dangers that arise when conservative Christians retreat from political activism. We give up our personal independence, sacrifice our religious liberties, and fail to lead the next generation by example and, ultimately, preserve their freedoms.

Believe me, I had to learn these lessons from someone, or I never would have found my way back from all the leftist misinformation I received about God and government. Thankfully my evangelical role model and mentor Wendy Wright, the current vice president of government relations for the Catholic Family and Human Rights Institute (C-FAM), led by example when she explained, "If we want to be free to evangelize through broadcasting, raise children with Biblical beliefs, to run businesses that honor God, to give to charities that we believe will do the best work, then we've got to restrain government...." Wendy wisely continued, "We've got to elect and place into key positions just and righteous people who ensure that we will have just laws that are applied equally."[2]

Character Counts

Eight days after Americans elected their president in 2012, it was reported that nearly 6.4 million evangelicals cast their vote for Barack Hussein Obama II[3]—a proven supporter of taxpayer-funded abortions who voted *three times*[4] to continue the horrific practice of partial-birth abortions, an advocate for same-sex marriage, an expander of the national debt, a national security risk-taker, and a religious liberty compromiser.

America's future looks pretty dim when evangelicals elect to the United States' highest seat of power a leader whose policies blatantly conflict with God's Word, the blueprint that determines how we live. Yet I hear my fellow churchgoers wonder aloud, "What's going wrong with our country?"

Have evangelicals forgotten that it's OK to seek godly leaders? Have we forgotten that it's OK to let biblical principles guide government policies? Our nation's founders encouraged it. James Madison, the fourth president of the United States, was spot-on when he said, "No people ought to feel greater obligations to celebrate the goodness of the Great Disposer of Events and the Destiny of Nations than the people of the United States."[5]

I can't help but worry that American evangelicals are taking for granted our blessed opportunity to elect officials whose actions reflect our Christian values. Sinful acts committed in office or codified through legislation could have serious social implications. This is not a responsibility we can afford to take lightly. And yet Christians are electing representatives whose personal and public personas directly conflict with biblical principles.

Of course, no man or woman is without blemish. Only Jesus fit that bill, and He didn't resemble a shiny, smooth-talking politician. So we have to get past the bright smiles and nice-sounding rhetoric to examine candidates' real character.

In an opinion article for Fox News, Penny Nance, president and CEO of Concerned Women for America, advised, "When a man or a woman chooses to run for public office, what they do in their private lives suddenly has public consequences. Isn't the truest test of character what you do when no one is watching?"[6]

It's not just the character of elected officials that count. Quite frankly Christlike character modeled at home may do more to affect the trajectory of this nation than you might think. On their own, 6.4 million evangelicals were not a large enough voting bloc to secure President Obama's second term in the White House. Can you guess which bracket of voters ultimately decided the 2012 presidential race? You're right if you guessed America's youth.

According to the Center for Information and Research on Civic Learning and Engagement, a whopping 67 percent of national voters between the ages of eighteen to twenty-nine voted for President Obama. The youth vote ultimately tipped the scales by giving President Obama majorities in the key battleground states of Virginia, Florida, Ohio, and Pennsylvania.[7]

These young voters were white, black, Southern, Northern, atheists, and yes, evangelical. Their backgrounds and experiences crossed a wide spectrum, but their shared political convictions ultimately led to four years of moral decline in America because they chose a candidate whose policies do not reflect biblical teaching.

Our Character Counts Too

In 1790 George Washington expressed the importance of personal character in a letter he wrote to his nephew, stating, "A good moral character is the first essential in a man."[8] Washington did not say good moral character is essential in a political man. This simple principle speaks volumes to not only politicians but also to pastors and parents.

Dale Hudson, a children's ministry expert, wrote a telling editorial that explored why pastors' kids especially are leaving the faith. Using data from the Barna Group, the nation's leading faith-based research organization, Hudson noted that 33 percent of pastors report that their children are no longer active in church.[9] The reasons were shocking.

According to Barna Group, 28 percent of pastors' kids struggle with their faith because of unrealistic expectations placed on them. But I was mostly struck that 14 percent of pastors' kids said faith was not consistently modeled at home.[10] The phrase "at home" is key in this study. Young evangelicals watch and learn from the actions taken behind the scenes. Role models' character in private can impact not only a young person's faith but also his or her civic responsibility.

Evangelicals and Government *Do* Mix

Those seeking to control the next generation of voters are not shooting in the dark, hoping their arrows hit the right target and that one day America's youth will vote their way. Their efforts are targeted, and they are taking aim while the rising generation is still very young.

While your children are still in school, secular society is training them to believe God has no place in government and that societies must be secular in order to fairly govern all people. God is viewed as a troublemaker who should be expelled from public schools and any other government-run entity—and never allowed back. Children learn from an early age that socializing with God on school grounds could land them in trouble.

Public schools banned Bible reading and recitation of the Lord's Prayer in 1963, but because faith is not so easy to expel, today there are watchdog groups such as the American Civil Liberties Union (ACLU) dedicated to removing God from all spheres of government. Todd Starnes of Fox News reported in November 2013 that the American Humanist Association (AHA) sued a Missouri public school teacher for allegedly praying over an injured student.[11] A Pennsylvania teacher was fired for simply showing his Bible to a student who had asked several times where the verse, "The last will be first, and the first will be last" was found.[12] The list of examples goes on. (We will revisit these infringements on religious freedoms in chapter 8.)

The assault on faith is relentless in schools. And sadly (and some might add unbelievably) left-leaning evangelical groups are coming alongside groups such as the ACLU and AHA to denounce Christians who express their faith on school grounds. Take, for example, the Baptist Joint Committee for Religious Liberty (BJC), a group whose mission is to segregate the church from the state. The BJC responded with disapproval after a North Carolina high school coach was found praying with his team. According to BJC blogger Don Byrd, the coach was also "proselytizing" (a negative way to say evangelizing) his team:

> Could a coach today not realize that leading his team in prayer and pushing them to accept Christ is an overstep?

Either way, good on [fellow coach] Capps for hearing and understanding the problem. Too many of these stories end with *defiance* and *lawsuits*.[13]

Prayer, evangelizing, and public school? Oh, my! Seriously though, the BJC's example raises an important question: What do Christians who refuse to fall in line with the Left do when our government's commandments conflict with God's? We cannot dismiss what the apostle Paul tells us in Romans 13:1, to "be subject to the governing authorities. For there is no authority except from God, and the authorities that exist are appointed by God" (NKJV). This message is echoed in the words of the apostle Peter:

> Be subject for the Lord's sake to every human institution, whether it be to the emperor as supreme, or to governors as sent by him to punish those who do evil and to praise those who do good. For this is the will of God, that by doing good you should put to silence the ignorance of foolish people.
>
> —1 PETER 2:13–15

Jesus made this clear when the Pharisees attempted to trip Him up with a trick question about paying taxes to the oppressive Roman government. Jesus answered them, "'Whose likeness and inscription is this?' They said, 'Caesar's.' Then he said to them, 'Therefore render to Caesar the things that are Caesar's, and to God the things that are God's" (Matt. 22:19–21).

Oftentimes the evangelical Left will try to remove Christian principles from the state while promoting the expansion of the federal government's power. But when Caesar encroaches upon God, the apostle Peter was clear that "we must obey God rather than men" (Acts 5:29).

There are significant parallels between the world's Christians and those long ago who were brought before public officials and told to denounce Christ. Sometimes we think about the men and women in the Bible as heroes with superpowers. The truth is, they were average people who faced the normal fears and anxieties that come with standing up against a government that opposes Christ. The Bible specifically states that Peter and John were considered common, uneducated men (Acts 4:13). The only thing that made them exceptional was their faith and prayers for boldness to confront their government and religious leaders:

> And when they heard it, they lifted their voices together to God and said… "And now, Lord, look upon their threats and grant to your servants to continue to speak your word with all boldness, while you stretch out your hand to heal, and signs and wonders are performed through the name of your holy servant Jesus." And when they had prayed, the place in which they were gathered together was shaken, and they were all filled with the Holy Spirit and continued to speak the word of God with boldness.
>
> —ACTS 4:24, 29–31

The pro-life movement is an example of Christians standing up for God's law over man's. According to the government, the murder of innocent unborn babies is lawful. Yet God instructs us not to murder in Exodus 20:13. Christians are also called to defend those who can't defend themselves, as Proverbs 31:8 instructs, "Open your mouth for the mute, for the rights of all who are destitute." Therefore Christians must continue to denounce this murder, even though abortion is legal.

The Great Commission also cannot be ignored despite prohibitions against "proselytizing." Before ascending into heaven, Jesus gave clear instructions to every believer:

> Go therefore and make disciples of all nations, baptizing them in the name of the Father and of the Son and of the

Holy Spirit, teaching them to observe all that I have commanded you.

—MATTHEW 28:19–20

So, I don't know about the BJC group, but when it boils down
to "defying" either God or Caesar, this evangelical girl is going
to continue following the Great Commission and live out the
instructions in 1 Timothy 4:13: "Until I come, devote yourself to
the public reading of Scripture, to exhortation, to teaching."

Why We Hold His Truths

The problem with groups such as the ACLU and BJC is that they
sorely misinterpret the "separation of church and state" metaphor, which, by the way, is found nowhere in the Declaration of
Independence or the Constitution.

In 1802 Founding Father Thomas Jefferson did reference a
"wall of separation" in his letter to the Danbury, Connecticut,
Baptist Association. However, Jefferson's statement was affirming
the church's protection from the state. He was not advocating for
the removal of all things Christian from the bedrock of government. Helping to shed some light on Jefferson's misunderstood
metaphor, Daniel L. Dreisbach, American University professor
of justice, law, and society, wrote: "Throughout his public career,
including two terms as President, Jefferson pursued policies
incompatible with the 'high and impregnable' wall the modern
Supreme Court has erroneously attributed to him. For example,
he endorsed the use of federal funds to build churches and to
support Christian missionaries working among the Indians.
The absurd conclusion that countless courts and commentators
would have us reach is that Jefferson routinely pursued policies
that violated his own 'wall of separation.'"[14]

Remember, the Ten Commandments were etched into the
very architecture of government buildings. And in 1802 when
Jefferson penned his "wall of separation" phrase, the Christian

book *Pilgrim's Progress* was read alongside the Bible as school textbooks, and prayers were offered in public schools. You can be sure that if the founders felt these public displays of faith "threatened" the public's welfare, they would have declared them unconstitutional.

Oftentimes my fellow pro-life, pro-family advocates and I are seen as a "threat" and are accused of wanting to take America back to the 1950s. My typical response is, "I'm twenty-six years old. I have no idea what the fifties were like. I'm just trying to bring America back to the Word of God."

Instead of removing Christian principles from the public realm, America's Founding Fathers relied heavily upon them. It is undeniable that prayer and the Bible are pillars of the United States. Patrick Henry said, "It is when a people forget God that tyrants forge their chains."[15]

Some contemporary national leaders also have had the courage to recognize that Christian teaching is a cornerstone in American politics. Former US Attorney General John Ashcroft correctly pointed out during a 1999 speech that, "Unique among the nations, America recognized the source of our character as being godly and eternal, not being civic and temporal. And because we have understood that our source is eternal, America has been different. We have no king but Jesus."[16]

Recognizing that there are certain things the government does not have the ability to create or interfere in, such as life and marriage, the founders drew from Judeo-Christian principles as the base for the freedoms outlined in the Declaration of Independence:

> We hold these truths to be self-evident, that all men are created equal, that they are endowed by their Creator with certain unalienable Rights, that among these are Life, Liberty and the pursuit of Happiness.[17]

Critics will say the truths found in the Bible are not exactly "self-evident" since they are written in black and white. But I would argue that to the founders it was obvious that life and liberty were sacred principles that no prosperous nation could ever neglect. They knew that a government needed to stand on a foundation of solid principles or it would collapse. Our nation's second president, John Adams, said, "It is Religion and Morality alone, which can establish the Principles upon which Freedom can securely stand."[18]

America's founders understood that power is tempting and we human beings are innately corrupt. For these reasons they built an ingenious governing system upon a series of checks and balances to ensure accountability—a word we evangelicals know well.

This system of checks and balances is made up of three branches of government: the executive branch (the president), the legislative branch (the Senate and House of Representatives), and the judicial (the Supreme Court). On top of these branches America has three levels of government: the federal or national level, the state level, and the local level. All the various branches and levels work together to keep everyone in check.

Americans live in a free society because upholding Judeo-Christian truths has spiritual and public policy benefits. The psalmist tells us, "Blessed is the nation whose God is the LORD, the people whom he has chosen as his heritage!" (Ps. 33:12). And I don't mean to frighten you, but Isaiah points out, "For the nation and kingdom that will not serve you shall perish; those nations shall be utterly laid waste" (Isa. 60:12).

The Ten Commandments are not engrained in America's oldest courtrooms for mere aesthetics. At the time of America's founding, the Ten Commandments were commonly held as a standard of right and wrong. Our national leaders knew their Bibles and understood that the Ten Commandments were guidelines that God handed down to Moses on Mount Sinai to establish the new nation of Israel. They believed that if the commandments were keys to Israel's blessing, they were keys to America's prosperity as well.

The civic benefits of honoring the Ten Commandments are indeed self-evident. The commandment to be truthful ensures a civil public discourse and functioning economy. Honoring one's father and mother and not coveting what your neighbor has are reasonable guidelines for building strong families. In his ten-segment series "Self-Evident Truths" CWA legal counsel Mario Diaz, Esq., noted that even honoring the Sabbath strengthens our nation. Diaz wrote:

> Even in today's materialistic, selfish age we can still recognize that there is more to life than the pursuit of the material. The Founders wrote about "the pursuit of happiness," a phrase that encompasses the whole of life. How many times do we hear of those who spent their entire lives trying to reach the top of the material mountain, just to learn, once they get there, that "the top" is not only just as unfulfilling as the base, but it is also a lot lonelier?[19]

God was clear that we should have no other gods but Him or He would "lay the sins of the parents upon their children; the entire family is affected—even children in the third and fourth generations of those who reject me" (Exod. 20:5, NLT).

Jesus said all the commandments could be summed up with two simple instructions: love God with all your heart, soul, mind, and strength; and love your neighbor as yourself (Matt. 22:37–40). Believing that it is right for us to love our neighbors (and even our enemies) is vital for the government to maintain peace, protect human rights, and administer justice according to the US Constitution.

Consider what our country would look like if our Founding Fathers weren't guided by the belief that we should love and respect others even when they hold opinions differing from our own. (See Matthew 5:43–48.) The Constitution might not preserve our freedom of religion, speech, or press. The United States might look similar to North Korea, an atheist regime that, according to BBC News, "sees organised religious activity as a potential challenge to the leadership."[20] Or America might resemble Iran, an Islamic republic that enforces oppressive Sharia law. The US Department of State reported that Iranians who deny the Islamic faith face harassment, intimidation, and discrimination.[21]

I agree with RenewAmerica analyst Ronald Cherry, MD, who wrote in *American Thinker,* "The values of Fascism, Nazism, Communism or Totalitarian Islamic Sharia Law for example must never metastasize in our American Culture, which traditionally has been Judeo-Christian." Cherry continued, "These Judeo-Christian Values should be kept central to the American spirit and culture even as we have become more multi-ethnic.... We must recognize that our culture, too, is worth preserving."[22]

The Future Christian-Politics Landscape

If America really is going through a post-Christian era as the evangelical Left so often says, conservative Christians must issue a clarion call for the nation to return to the biblical principles our country was founded upon. This is the only way we can preserve America's prosperity and freedoms. Mull over Matthew 5:16 for a moment: "Let your light shine before others, so that they may see your good works and give glory to your Father who is in heaven."

Should the next generation of evangelicals choose either the couch-potato, "stay out of it," route or the evangelical Left's cafeteria-style, "pick and choose," Christianity, America as the land of liberty is in serious trouble. Both paths lead to Christians' handing over our religious freedoms. Both paths give up on our being a "beacon of hope" or "salt and light" to the world.

Grown-ups, there are two major steps you can take to help steer America back to its founding Christian principles. First, lead by example. Pastors and teachers, while the IRS does not allow you to endorse candidates, you are able to discuss the importance of supporting people (elected or not) who demonstrate godly character. And parents, be sure to vote—and talk with your kids about the principles that guide your voting decisions. Discuss the culture wars and explain that God and government constantly collide, and we must serve God over mere men.

Second, and I can't stress this enough, pray. First Timothy 2:1–2 instructs: "I urge that supplications, prayers, intercessions, and thanksgivings be made for all people, for kings and all who are in high positions, that we may lead a peaceful and quiet life, godly and dignified in every way." To complete that task well, Christians must stay abreast of the national challenges. As a pastor once said, we should pray with a Bible in one hand and a newspaper in the other.

The presidency of the United States is one of the most difficult and important jobs on the earth. We must pray for whoever is in office to receive wisdom and direction that will ensure American's well-being.

Likewise, every day our nine Supreme Court justices make complex legal decisions that impact the entire nation. We should stay informed so that we can pray that God grants them wisdom and courage to uphold our Constitution on specific issues. Isaiah reminds us that "the LORD is our judge; the LORD is our lawgiver; the LORD is our king; he will save us" (Isa. 33:22).

Finally, we must lift up the United States Senate and House of Representatives. We must pray that the 535 elected officials lead with truthfulness and righteousness. We must pray that they come to acknowledge God's ultimate authority so that His will is carried out in our state houses, courtrooms, and public school systems.

A quote that brings all that we've discussed into clear view is often attributed to Alexis de Tocqueville, the man who toured America in 1831 to uncover what made the country so great. After his tour, de Tocqueville is said to have made a haunting prediction about America's future should her citizens ever abandon our biblical truths. He is quoted as saying:

> I sought for the greatness and genius of America in her commodious harbors and her ample rivers—and it was not there...in her fertile fields and boundless forests and it was not there...in her rich mines and her vast world commerce—and it was not there...in her democratic Congress and her matchless Constitution—and it was not there. Not until I went into the churches of America and heard her pulpits aflame with righteousness did I understand the secret of her genius and power. America is great because she is good, and if America ever ceases to be good, she will cease to be great.[23]

America needs evangelical Christians who will speak out against the cafeteria-style Christianity that threatens the biblical principles our exceptional country was founded upon. America needs you, because as President Ronald Reagan said, "Freedom is a fragile thing and never more than one generation away from extinction. It is not ours by inheritance; it must be fought for and defended constantly by each generation."[24]

Chapter 3

EMERGING FROM
THE EMERGENT MOVEMENT

> *Don't ever take a fence down until*
> *you know the reason it was put up.*[1]
>
> G. K. CHESTERTON

HO IS BRIAN MCLAREN?" I REMEMBER THINKING BACK in 2007. A naïve college student, I could not have foreseen what this name would represent to me and millions of other Millennials by 2014. I had just plugged in to a popular ministry on Virginia Tech's campus. It was a wildly popular interdenominational campus church that steered clear of complex and controversial Christian teachings. It was here that I first came into contact with the evangelical Left.

My newfound friends were telling me about the three campus pastors who led the nearly eight hundred Christian students who attended the church. One of the pastors was in talks with Zondervan to publish a book about God and tragedy. You see, just a few months before this conversation, on April 16, a student opened fire on campus, killing thirty-two people and wounding seventeen. The university was still struggling through shock and heartbreak.

My friends were thrilled, and rightly so, about their pastor's book deal. Through Zondervan this young, gifted minister had the opportunity to not only write but also to connect with other published authors. One of these authors was a key leader within the evangelical Left, Brian McLaren. I was told that McLaren and our campus pastor had become fast friends, establishing a sort of mentor-mentee relationship. In the moment this sounded exciting, as if I were witnessing the beginning of something big. In time the connection would prove even more significant because McLaren's liberal ideas would influence some of the campus staff, then the small group leaders, and eventually me.

To be clear, there were no emergent classes offered at this campus ministry, no blatant liberal creeds in the sermon and no instructions to vote for Obama. The evangelical Left is cleverer with their language. Instead, words such as *tolerance, nonconforming,* and *liberated* made their way into Bible studies and everyday conversations. Of course, the morality of abortion, same-sex relationships, and religious liberty went undiscussed. We were taught to define our faith by our work in the community. Words such as *sin, hell, transformation,* and *authority* were rarely spoken.

Completely unprepared to spot distorted Christian teachings and in fear of being ostracized, I ignored the warnings that clearly resonate in Paul's letter to the Romans:

> I appeal to you, brothers, to watch out for those who cause divisions and create obstacles contrary to the doctrine that you have been taught; avoid them. For such persons do not serve our Lord Christ, but their own appetites, and by smooth talk and flattery they deceive the hearts of the naive.
>
> —Romans 16:17–18

Soon I started to embrace a liberal Christian paradigm. I started fighting with my mom and dad over the Bible's acceptance of same-sex relationships. I ardently believed in a faux gender war within certain evangelical denominations. Convinced that big government and expanded welfare programs were a prerequisite for evangelism, I even started to use social justice jargon.

To be sure, I still identified as an evangelical. Only now I was an evangelical holding on to principles that swerved away from the Bible.

What Does an Evangelical Look Like?

If I ask you to close your eyes and envision an evangelical, you would probably imagine a middle-aged American who wears casual slacks to his nondenominational megachurch. Am I right? But identifying evangelicals is not as easy as that. If we peel back all the layers of evangelicalism, we discover a rich history, a complicated present, and an even more troubling future.

Americans tend to view the term *evangelical* as being birthed out of the Billy Graham era and labeling such leaders as Jerry Falwell and James Dobson. However, this word was used in the sixteenth century to designate Protestant denominations during the Reformation. It was recycled again in the nineteenth century when "evangelical" identified ministers such as British pastor Charles H. Spurgeon, missionary J. Hudson Taylor, and Calvinist theologian and Dutch politician Abraham Kuyper.[2] Sadly, this "age of the evangelical" virtually flatlined after the 1870s because humanism began to flourish in Western societies.

Evangelicalism was muted but only for a while. After coming face-to-face with sheer evil during World War II, the world was brought to its knees and began relying once again upon its Creator for hope and peace. Shortly afterward passionate ministers such as Billy Graham emerged on the scene, as did Bible colleges and Christian media such as the Christian Broadcasting

Network (CBN) and *Christianity Today* magazine. All of this evolved into what we now know as American evangelicalism.[3]

I've struggled for years to find a precise definition of *evangelical* or *evangelicalism*. Trust me when I tell you that the myriad definitions will make your head spin. The best, clear-cut definition I have discovered was in the book *The Young Evangelicals: Revolution in Orthodoxy*. In it author Richard Quebedeaux uses three criteria to identify an evangelical: (1) evangelicals identify the full authority of Scripture in all matters of faith and practice; (2) evangelicals pursue a personal faith in Jesus Christ as Lord and Savior; and (3) evangelicals understand the urgency of seeking the conversion of sinful men and women to Christ.[4] But these criteria still aren't enough. Not everyone who wears the evangelical label actually advocates *everything* Jesus taught. They meet the three criteria but pick and choose which teachings to emphasize.

A better means of identifying evangelicals is found in the Gospel of Matthew:

> You will recognize them by their fruits. Are grapes gathered from thornbushes, or figs from thistles? So, every healthy tree bears good fruit, but the diseased tree bears bad fruit. A healthy tree cannot bear bad fruit, nor can a diseased tree bear good fruit. Every tree that does not bear good fruit is cut down and thrown into the fire. Thus you will recognize them by their fruits.
>
> —MATTHEW 7:16–20

On C-SPAN's *Washington Journal*, guest Janice Shaw Crouse, PhD, the senior fellow of the Beverly LaHaye Institute and my friend, was pointedly asked, "Do you believe that President Obama is a Christian?" It was supposed to be sort of a stump question.

Crouse responded: "President Obama says he is a Christian.

There are rhetorical Christians, political Christians—all sorts of Christians. It is very easy to say you are a Christian. We do believe in looking at Christians' lives to see whether they put action behind their words and whether their attitudes and . . . their values reflect their beliefs."[5]

The "New Evangelicals"

Recognizing evangelicals "by their fruits" just got a whole lot trickier. One critic colorfully identified the problem facing Christianity in America. In his book *Bad Religion* author and *New York Times* contributor Ross Douthat writes, "America's problem isn't too much religion, or too little of it. It's *bad* religion: the slow-motion collapse of traditional Christianity and the rise of a variety of destructive pseudo-Christianities in its place."[6]

The problem Douthat diagnosed is a growing movement within evangelicalism that is coined "new evangelicalism." But there is really nothing new about it. This movement is doing little more than repackaging an old brand of leftist Christianity to Millennials. As the saying goes, "You can put lipstick on a pig, but it's still a pig."

The "new evangelicals" are simply the twenty-first-century face of the 1960s evangelical Left. This small but vocal and influential group paints themselves as a hip, fresh, young group of evangelicals rising against patriarchy, wealth, and privilege. Yet the movement is steered by the same Left-leaning evangelicals we've known for years, including the granddaddy of the evangelical Left, Jim Wallis. Founder of the group Sojourners, Wallis remains a leading voice in the über-liberal emergent movement along with Brian McLaren, prominent evangelical lobbyist Richard Cizik, and evangelical ethicist David Gushee—all middle-aged, successful white men, mind you.

Sometimes referred to as "progressive Christians," the

evangelical Left began as a well-intentioned force challenging sexism, racism, and economic injustice. Yet fast-forward to today, and the new evangelicals have centered their theology around:

- The church's acceptance of lesbian, gay, bisexual, and transgender (LGBT) lifestyles

- The questioning of Scripture's unfailing authority

- "Liberating" women from their supposed oppression in the church and home

- Promoting mass legalization of illegal immigrants

- Thwarting climate change

- Expanding the federal "nanny" state

If you are thinking that this "theology" sounds less like Scripture and more like the Democratic National Committee (DNC) platform, then you're not alone.

Ironically the evangelical Left's marketing pitch to young evangelicals is that they are not political, polarizing, or controversial. According to its mission statement, Jim Wallis's group Sojourners "builds alliances among, and mobilizes people of faith, focusing on racial and social justice, life and peace, and environmental stewardship."[7]

Cizik, president of the New Evangelical Partnership for the Common Good (NEP), stated his group's position this way: "We are committed to not politicizing the church....We are for vigorous dialogue within the evangelical church about what constitutes the 'common good,' and the pursuit of that end, but we do not want the church wracked by politics."[8]

Speaking on behalf of young evangelicals, popular blogger and author Rachel Held Evans throws out the false claim that young Christians are leaving the church because Christianity has become "too political, too exclusive, old-fashioned, unconcerned

with social justice and hostile to lesbian, gay, bisexual and transgender people." So in her CNN op-ed, she advocates for churches
to become less concerned with the culture wars and more con-
sumed with making "our LGBT friends to feel truly welcome in
our faith communities"; holiness is not just about sexual purity,
she writes, but also about caring for the poor, the environment,
and the oppressed.[9]

Pretending they steer clear of American politics, the evangelical Left tells Millennials that the James Dobsons and Beverly
LaHayes of the world are working against progress because they
insist on using only the Bible as a guideline for ethical and moral
governance in a pluralistic society. Their views and approach to
public policy are polarizing, they argue, and void of the love and
acceptance Jesus modeled.

Seems odd, doesn't it? Professing Christians telling young
Christians to shun other Christians who advocate for Christian
principles in public policy. (How dare we, Christians!) The reason
the evangelical Left would take such a stance is because despite
how "apolitical" they claim to be, this liberal movement has its
own radical and, yes, political agenda.

I pointed out the Left's double standards in my article "Why
Liberal Evangelicals Are Lying to Millennials."[10] I wrote the piece
back in 2013 after New Jersey Sen. Cory Booker was a featured
speaker at the Atlanta Catalyst conference, a Christian gathering
aimed at young people. Booker's biography on the conference
website did not even mention the words *God, Jesus,* or *Christian.*
I found no testimony of salvation, but there were plenty of liberal
platitudes.

Booker may not be known for his relationship with Christ, but
he certainly is known for advocating taxpayer-funded abortions
regardless of the infringements on religious liberties. Could it be
that someone was attempting to be clever and hoped to spread a
liberal worldview among the unsuspecting conference attendees

by slotting Senator Booker between prominent evangelicals such as John Piper and Priscilla Shirer?

In addition to supporting liberal candidates, the evangelical Left welcomes support from the secular left wing. Jim Wallis's organization, Sojourners, accepted a $200,000 grant from leftist billionaire George Soros in 2004, another $100,000 in 2007, and $150,000 in 2011.[11] An atheist, Soros is also a proud bankroller of secular humanist agendas, including abortion, same-sex marriage, the United Nation's control over gun ownership, and anti-Israel initiatives.[12] What's worse is that when *World* magazine reported on Soros's funding of the Christian nonprofit, Wallis initially denied the reports before finally coming clean and apologizing for his attempted coverup.[13]

Beyond liberal political activism, the most unique characteristic of the evangelical Left is their biblical criticism. Many within the evangelical Left believe the Bible is not to be taken literally but metaphorically because of its "flaws." In other words, they believe the Bible was not divinely inspired but has been influenced by men and culture and therefore should be loosely interpreted. Not all will come out and say that, perhaps in an attempt to avoid being labeled sacrilegious. The *New Evangelical Manifesto* states that "new evangelicals" recognize the authority of Scripture, even though some of its contributors affirm homosexuality. At least progressive Christian Roger Wolsey was honest when he wrote: "We don't think that God wrote the Bible. We think it was written by fallible human beings who were inspired by (not dictated to by) the Holy Spirit. Hence, we don't consider it to be infallible or inerrant."[14]

This view that Scripture is "flawed" clashes with evangelicals' belief that the Bible is divinely inspired. It also conflicts with 2 Timothy 3:16–17:

> All Scripture is God-breathed and is useful for teaching, rebuking, correcting and training in righteousness, so that

the servant of God may be thoroughly equipped for every
good work.

—NIV

Though many in the evangelical Left reject Scripture's authority,
a central theme is Micah 6:8, which instructs, "He has told you,
O man, what is good; and what does the LORD require of you
but to do justice, and to love kindness, and to walk humbly with
your God?"

Using this verse, the Left lifts community over Christian
teachings and views themselves as champions of the oppressed
while simultaneously portraying conservative Christians as con-
sumed with power and greed. Brian McLaren defined pro-family
conservative Christians as those who "supported wars of choice,
defended torture, opposed environmental protection, and
seemed to care more about protecting the rich....They wanted
to protect unborn human life inside the womb, but didn't seem
to care about born human life in slums or prisons."[15]

Pardon me, but it is worth traveling down a short rabbit trail
here to note America's largest prison ministry, Prison Fellowship.
Interestingly this ministry was started by Charles Colson, one of
those pro-family Christian extremists McLaren warned us about.

The criticisms from the evangelical Left are just as hurtful and
judgmental as they allege the claims of their traditional counterparts are. While I cannot speak for other conservative Christians,
I certainly do not work for a Christian nonprofit for the power or
money. My fellow pro-family Christians enter this area of ministry accepting the fact that funding is scarce and glory is absent.
All of us professional, pro-family culture warriors check our
earthly wealth at the door and pray that each year we will raise
enough funding to continue our ministries and pay our rent. If
I wanted power and money, I would go work for a George Soros–
funded organization.

The Emergent Movement

Chances are that you have heard of the "emergent church movement" or the "emerging movement." If you haven't heard these terms, grab a pen and paper and let's take notes.

According to a study by the Lutheran Church—Missouri Synod, the emergent movement refers to doctrinally liberal Christian leaders and communities. The emerging movement is a term for so-called "progressive" Christian communities that follow a biblically conservative but less traditional church model.[16] To be sure, it is the emergent movement that you have to worry about.

The emergent movement is something of a subgroup of the evangelical Left. For example, Brian McLaren is a founding member of the emergent movement but also a prominent member of the evangelical Left. Note that not all members of the evangelical Left are part of the emergent church. For example, Jim Wallis is part of the evangelical Left but has never identified as emergent. Still, their politics and theology align, and because of how loosely organized the emergent movement is, the evangelical Left is adopting it into its ranks.

For nearly twenty years the emergent movement has been largely a disorganized venture without definite boundaries and limits. This makes it extremely difficult to identify emergent evangelicals, unless you have a clear understanding of the emergent movement's foundations, transformation, and unique characteristics.

An account of emergent history is best told by Pastor Mark Driscoll, a former and founding member of the movement. According to Driscoll, the emerging idea first surfaced in the mid-1990s at a Christian conference in Seattle. The conference focused on reshaping the church's outreach methods in an attempt to appeal to the emerging generations that no longer identified with the worship styles of the baby boomer generation. After the conference a small group of pioneers continued to work to develop a new model for outreach. The "missional church," as it came to be called, asserted that church leaders should view Western society as its own mission field and "meet people where they are" instead of expecting non-Christians to walk into their churches from off the street.[17]

Soon the teaching of the missional church morphed into something doctrinally disturbing. Instead of upholding the Bible as God's infallible Word, the small group believed Christians should challenge the authority of Scripture. By May of 2001 the group included six church leaders: Brian McLaren at the helm, Doug Pagitt, Tim Keel, Chris Seay, Tim Conder, and Brad Cecil. These men became the first "emergents."[18]

By this time Driscoll had departed from the pack due to its abandonment of orthodox Christian teaching. Dan Kimball too was a leading voice in the early emergent movement, but like Driscoll he was concerned by the movement's abandonment of traditional teaching. Kimball said, "When the whole emerging church discussion began, it was primarily about evangelism and mission to emerging generations. That's why I got into it, and it was fun and a thrill to be part of."[19]

Kimball went on to acknowledge, "A lot of the things discussed and then even becoming beliefs is pretty liberal theology. My concern is seeing younger Christians especially who don't know these theological issues were discussed before and the results of the discussions throughout Church history get caught up in thinking this is a new expression of Christianity when it is pretty much classical extreme liberalism in a new, cooler wrapper."[20]

Answering the question "What concerns you most about the emergent church?" theologian John Piper said, "The single greatest concern for me is their attitude towards doctrine." He continued, "The issue is their attitude towards truth. I'm deeply concerned about it, and I think that it will be the undoing of the emergent church as it has come to be. They don't believe that truth itself is an objective propositional thing that has a yes and a no. Nothing is ever either/or, good or bad, right or wrong, ugly or beautiful. It's all vague."[21]

What I can tell you is that the emergent movement is designed, just like the evangelical Left, to appeal to Millennials by touting a need to rebel against tradition and privilege—the same jargon students are force-fed in college classrooms. The emergent movement is anti-capitalism, as the entrepreneurial spirit of our parents and grandparents is deemed greedy and uncompassionate. Patriotism is seen as oppressive and ignorant, and American Christian missionaries are often viewed as white imperial colonizers.

Central to this movement are "cohorts," which are gatherings to discuss creative liberal theology and semantics. The only central structure is the Emergent Village, comprised of a group of volunteers who coordinate the cohorts nationwide. In an effort to move away from traditional church buildings and membership, emergents establish cohorts in their local coffeehouses, homes, or bars rather than in sanctuaries.[22] Instead of traditional sermons grounded in Scripture and Christian teaching, emergent communities emphasize conversations about faith.

Unwittingly in college I became what I call an emergent evangelical, but only for a short period of time. Thank God, I had valiant Christian mentors who refused to give up on me. My parents, Christian teachers, and pro-family leaders helped guide me back to understanding God's absolute truth.

The Lord might also impress a sense of duty on your heart to safeguard young believers by honestly discussing their challenges and acknowledging their questions. Or perhaps you are the student who finds it tough to stand alone but something within your heart and mind tells you compromise is not an option. If either of those scenarios describes you, chew on these instructions found in Colossians: "See to it that no one takes you captive by philosophy and empty deceit, according to human tradition, according to the elemental spirits of the world, and not according to Christ" (Col. 2:8).

Voices of a Movement

There are numerous books, bloggers, and Christian college and conference speakers who reflect liberal theology and are influencing this generation. Indeed, knowing where to start getting acquainted with these new influencers can be difficult. So as a helpful guide, I created the following list, which gives a brief overview of each leader's social and political witness:

Paul Alexander

A former Assemblies of God clergyman, Paul Alexander made several unorthodox claims that included liberation theology and endorsements of homosexuality while addressing the Society for Pentecostal Studies. The comments ultimately led to his dismissal. Alexander is the cofounder of Pentecostals and Charismatics for Peace and Justice and copresident of Evangelicals for Social Action (ESA), a left-leaning social justice group. Alexander promotes peacemaking and the building of American/international relationships. In an interview with the *Christian Post* Alexander asserted that new progressive evangelicalism "is a form of bringing to reality God's vision, God's hope for all of humanity."[23]

Jay Bakker

Son of the televangelists Jim and Tammy Faye Bakker, Jay Bakker is a cofounder of Revolution Church and a critic of traditional evangelicals. After years of drug rehabilitation, Bakker embraced a very radical, progressive style of Christianity.

Bakker's pastoral style focuses on grace and inclusion. In an interview with ABC News, Bakker said, "It sounds so churchy, but I felt like God spoke to my heart and said '[homosexuality] is not a sin.'"[24]

After Minnesota became the twelfth state to redefine marriage, Bakker marked the occasion by leading his church in "rainbow bread" communion. A longtime opponent of Christian political associations, Bakker explained the communion by saying, "Yeah, I'm gettin' political. This is to celebrate our LGBTQ brothers and sisters... [and remember] those who maybe didn't make it this far."[25]

Rob Bell

The former pastor of Mars Hill Bible Church and author of *Love Wins*, Rob Bell is among the most recognizable liberal thinkers within the evangelical Left. But as his faith in traditional Christian teachings waned, so did his flourishing ministry. Within a few years Bell's church went from ten thousand attenders to thirty-five hundred before he eventually left the church in 2011.[26]

Hopping on the "coexist" bandwagon, Bell claims there are alternative routes besides Jesus to salvation. Bell has stated, "I affirm the truth anywhere in any religious system, in any worldview. If it's true, it belongs to God."[27] In his first book, *Velvet Elvis*, he wrote, "So as a Christian, I am free to claim the good, the true, the holy, *wherever and whenever* I find it. I live with the understanding that truth is bigger than any religion and the world is God's and everything in it."[28] In 2014 Bell was to join Oprah Winfrey's aptly titled "The Life You Want" tour focusing on mystical aspects of faith and spirituality rather than the values and commandments outlined in Scripture.[29]

Nadia Bolz-Weber

Nadia Bolz-Weber's pastoral style combines liturgy and community, beer and hymns, foul language and sexual innuendos. All this is coupled with a determination to transcend the bounds of both the religious Right and liberal Left, making her a vibrant powerhouse for the evangelical Left.

Bolz-Weber sways away from her cohorts within the religious Left in that she does not believe in creating a "customer friendly" environment in order to attract young believers. While discussing her memoir, *Pastrix*, at Calvary Baptist in Washington DC in 2013, Bolz-Weber said, "If a community has a more 'progressive' ethos and is open and affirming, then they start to sort of soften the edges... [and] the proclamation of the gospel." Yet while affirming this "softening" of the gospel, she promotes Jesus and His gospel as "the only two things going for us." This is precisely what makes her appealing. As the *Washington Post* explained, she "merges the passion and life-changing fervor of evangelicalism with the commitment to inclusiveness and social justice of mainline Protestantism."[30] The problem is, inclusiveness, social justice, and "passion" don't have the power to change lives. Only the gospel does, without the "softening."

Tony Campolo

Baptist evangelist Tony Campolo is the founder of Red Letter Christians, a liberal Christian group that closed in June 2014.[31] Well-known in the political world, Campolo served as President Bill Clinton's spiritual adviser during the Monica Lewinsky scandal. While he professes to be pro-life and pro-traditional marriage, Campolo criticizes the politicization of Christianity while simultaneously peddling liberal political agendas in blogs and interviews.[32] Campolo recently urged President Obama to meet with North Korea's communist dictator and touts US disarmament. "If we want our enemies to dismantle nuclear weapons we should show them we're serious—by dismantling our own," Campolo said. "I contend we cannot expect others to do what we are not willing to do ourselves."[33]

Campolo has not stated that he supports homosexuality but argues that keeping government out of marriages would minimize conflict among parties. In an attempt at "compromise," Campolo wrote: "I propose that the government should get out of the business of marrying people and, instead, only give legal status to civil unions. The government should do this for both gay couples and straight couples, and leave marriage in the hands of the church and other religious entities. That's the way it works in Holland."[34] This "compromise" is a view also held by some conservatives. But the federal government relinquishing control over marriage is a slim possibility. So this "solution" is no real answer at all.

Richard Cizik

For nearly thirty years Richard Cizik worked as a lobbyist for the National Association of Evangelicals (NAE). He was forced to resign after promoting federally sanctioned same-sex unions during an interview with National Public Radio in 2008. Since then Cizik has helped launch the New Evangelical Partnership for the Common Good (NEP), which he considers a "new evangelical" movement.[35] In addition, Cizik focuses on merging his politics on climate change and controversial "family planning" initiatives with Christianity.

Shane Claiborne

Activist and author of *The Irresistible Revolution*, Shane Claiborne is an influential voice among young evangelicals who often emphasizes social justice over transformation and salvation through Jesus Christ. Claiborne founded The Simple Way, a faith-based commune in inner-city Philadelphia. If asked whether or not he is an evangelical, Shane will offer an evasive answer, "If by evangelical we mean one who spreads the good news that there is another kingdom or superpower, an economy and a peace other than that of the nations, a savior other than Caesar, then yes, I am an evangelical."[36] By this definition—which doesn't mention biblical authority, the urgency of witnessing, or even Jesus Christ by name—even our Jewish friends could identify as evangelical.

A pacifist, Claiborne often criticizes the United States and even its Christian roots. In *The Irresistible Revolution* he grossly mischaracterizes the Puritans, who fled Europe under religious persecution for America, writing, "Church history is filled with movements of piety, like the Puritans, who marked themselves by separating from the unholy and deemed it as their duty to *destroy all that is not pure* in the world."[37]

Claiborne seems to believe the United States has some fundamental flaws that have created an oppressive system called free-market capitalism. Without going so far as to say it is a sin to be rich, Claiborne advocates a redistribution of wealth and often implies that wealth is equivalent to greed: "Layers of insulation separate the rich and the poor from truly encountering one another. There are the obvious layers like picket fences and SUVs, and there are the more subtle ones like charity."[38]

Clearly, Claiborne has a genuine concern for the needy. The problem is that he suggests that having things is bad, whether those items are used for selfish or selfless purposes. Is it selfish and greedy when my mom uses her SUV (that she and my father worked and saved very hard to buy) to take her car-less church members to the grocery store each week? Of course not, because my parents are being good stewards of their possession in order to help those in need. And they refuse to brag about their actions. As the adage goes, "Don't judge a book by its cover," Shane.

Jennifer Crumpton

A self-proclaimed feminist evangelical and member of Cizik's NEP, Jennifer Crumpton frequently writes for Patheos's progressive blog channel advocating for taxpayer-funded contraception and abortion when necessary. About abortion she has said, "No one *wants* abortions. But life is extraordinarily complex and often very unfair to women, especially poor women, on many levels." She also wrote that women's "right to control our own bodies and make decisions about our own reproductive systems is an economic issue."[39] The major problem with Crumpton's seemingly compassionate, progressive ideology is that it views children as a burden unless they are deemed valuable by their parents.

Rachel Held Evans

A popular post-evangelical blogger and speaker, Rachel Held Evans rose in notoriety after the publication of her second book, *A Year of Biblical Womanhood*, in which she attempted to "follow all of the Bible's instructions for women as literally as possible for a year to show that no woman, no matter how devout, is actually practicing biblical womanhood all the way."[40] The purpose of Evans's experiment was not to call women to true biblical womanhood but to poke holes in the Bible's view of womanhood. Kathy Keller, wife of pastor and author Tim Keller, correctly pointed out the flaws in Evans's experiment in her honest, biblical review. "In making the decision to ignore the tectonic shift that occurred when Jesus came," Keller wrote, "you have led your readers not into a better understanding of biblical interpretation, but into a worse one. Christians don't arbitrarily ignore the Levitical code— they see it as wonderfully fulfilled in Jesus."[41]

A member of the so-called "Jesus Feminist" movement, Evans states that she is pro-life but is an ardent supporter of government-funded contraception. In her blog post "Privilege and the Pill" Evans claimed the high abortion rate in the United States is due to the difficulty women have obtaining contraceptives. "Birth control should be an important topic to those of us who consider ourselves pro-life," she wrote, "because the most effective way to curb the abortion rate in this country is to make birth control more affordable and accessible."[42] (We will see in chapter 7 that greater access to contraception does not necessarily reduce the number of abortions.)

Lynne Hybels

Lynne Hybels, wife of megachurch pastor Bill Hybels, is the author of *Nice Girls Don't Change the World*. Less known about Hybels is that she is a contributing editor for Jim Wallis's liberal activist group Sojourners. Hybels is also a leading pro-Palestinian activist within the church, as a statement in her blog indicates, "When I say I'm pro-Palestinian, I mean that I believe the Palestinians have an equally valid right to live in the land and should have the same civil rights that are afforded to Israeli Jewish citizens, whether that's in one state, two states, or however many states." Hybels states that she believes "it is possible to be truly pro-Israeli and pro-Palestinian at the same time."[43] Yet in terms of how to achieve the geopolitical peace she envisions, Hybels offers no clear solutions.

Tony Jones

Showing open aggression toward traditional Christian teachings, emergent movement writer Tony Jones is notorious for his politically charged ideas and moral relativism. Recently Jones has focused on changing Christian teaching on sexuality. In the wake of World Vision's effective same-sex "marriage" endorsement, subsequently followed by their reaffirmation of traditional marriage, Jones made an exceptionally off-base claim about Millennials. According to Jones, young evangelicals are "looking for—even hoping for—some advance on the issue of rights and love and equality for GLBT persons. That's what will keep them in the Christian faith."[44] In his short blog posts, Jones has attempted to erase the moral boundaries surrounding premarital sex, open marriages, and polyamory.[45] Jones wrote, "A new sexual ethic for Christians is desperately needed. I for one am going to work on that."[46]

Brian McLaren

Brian McLaren is a cofounder of the emergent movement and a leader within the evangelical Left. As I sat in a Washington DC–area seminar listening to McLaren promote his new book, I cringed when I heard him say, "Sin is a failure to grow. God wants us to keep growing."[47] Sin is much more than a failure to grow. We were born in sin. We didn't need Jesus to die for our sins because we refused to grow, but because our sinful state separated us from God. Jesus's death was the only way we could be reconciled to Him.

But McLaren doesn't see things quite that way. He believes salvation "is about God's ongoing work in creation to liberate from slavery, oppression, exploitation, lust, greed, pride, and all other forms of sin and evil." And Christianity "is a movement of people joining God in the healing of the world, beginning with ourselves, following the way of Jesus."[48] McLaren's views on homosexuality have evolved during his writing and speaking career. In 2012 McLaren's son Trevor Douglas McLaren married his same-sex partner. McLaren performed the ceremony.[49]

Carl Medearis

An "expert on Muslim-Christian relations" and author of *Speaking of Jesus: The Art of Not-Evangelism*, Carl Medearis likes to soften the reality of Islamic terrorism by painting groups such as Hezbollah as Jesus-endorsing nice guys. At the Simply Jesus conference in November 2013 he grossly misrepresented the terror ambitions of Hezbollah to his audience full of young evangelicals when he said: "So I'm speaking in a Shi'ite Muslim mosque in South Lebanon controlled by a group called Hezbollah. Hezbollah, or a Shi'ite Lebanese organization we'll say that do various things—you may have heard of them. And so, one of the things that you probably didn't know they do is they invited me to speak in their mosque. So, that didn't make it on Fox News."[50]

You may not have heard of that version of Hezbollah because that isn't the real Hezbollah. The real Hezbollah has terrorized both Jews and Christians in the Middle East. Faith McDonnell, IRD's director of Christian persecution programs, aptly pointed out that Carl Medearis may like "to break down paradigms by expressing his intimate relationship with Islamic groups like Hezbollah but regardless of what Medearis thinks, the current paradigm for most Christians in the Islam-dominated world is oppression and persecution. His tongue-in-cheek portrayal of Hezbollah as a 'Shi'ite Lebanese organization' could be considered disrespectful to their Israeli victims."[51]

Jim Wallis

President of the über-liberal evangelical activist group Sojourners, Jim Wallis is a spiritual adviser to President Obama and author of the widely popular book *God's Politics*. According to Wallis, it is the government's responsibility to make life fair for all. During a talk at the Brookings Institution in Washington DC on April 3, 2013, Wallis explained that after "biblical study" he concluded that according to "Romans 13 and all the rest...our human inclinations and human sins make things unfair inevitably, and so government is to make things more fair."[52]

During an interview with *Christianity Today*, Wallis said that young, theologically conservative evangelicals are "deserting the Religious Right in droves" because the evangelical community attempts to "restrict the language of 'moral values' to just two issues—abortion and gay marriage."[53] In terms of politics and Christianity, Wallis says, "I would suggest that the Bible is neither 'conservative' nor 'liberal' as we understand those terms in a political context today."[54] Yet Wallis has made his political agenda clear. He advocates maintaining legalized abortion, writing, "My public-policy view has a strong bias toward protecting unborn life in every possible way, but without criminalizing abortion."[55] And in 2013 Wallis officially endorsed same-sex marriage.[56]

The religious Left has a savvy way of convincing Millennials that to be compassionate and authentically Christian, one must conform to popular culture, inaccurately suggesting that is what it means to be missional. The truth is, Millennials within our evangelical communities must realize that Christianity is not an identity we slip on and off like a pair of shoes when it is comfortable. Our faith characterizes our recognition of the inerrant authority of Scripture, a personal relationship with Jesus Christ, and determination to publicly share the good news without cultural compromise.

PART TWO:
DIGGING INTO THE ISSUES

> *But in your hearts honor Christ the Lord as holy, always being prepared to make a defense to anyone who asks you for a reason for the hope that is in you; yet do it with gentleness and respect.*
>
> **1 PETER 3:15**

Chapter 4

CONFRONTING THE SAME-SEX DILEMMA

> *People drift along from generation to generation, and the morally unthinkable becomes thinkable as the years move on.*[1]
>
> FRANCIS SCHAEFFER

URING MY TIME AS A SUNDAY SCHOOL TEACHER, I'VE COME face-to-face with some unflinching jabber-jaws. These kids are witty, smart, and downright hilarious. They are America's future military men and women, political leaders, teachers, pastors, and parents. These kids are bold and willing to talk about every pop culture issue—except one.

All I have to do is whisper the word *gay*, and silence befalls my Sunday school classroom. Afraid to tread into "dangerous" territory, my students will lower their upraised hands, and their smiling faces turn to frowns as their eyes fall to the floor.

The same-sex debate easily tops America's list of controversial topics. In this arena intimidation and slander tactics flow freely.

Lawsuits can be filed against Americans who use gender-specific pronouns such as "she," "Sir," or "Miss," if they are deemed "unwelcome" by their recipient.[2] Political correctness muzzles even the boldest adults from entering the debate.

You might be thinking, "Why is she talking about such a controversial issue with middle-school kids?" The answer is, because they are already being taught to embrace the gay lifestyle.

As early as middle school (and probably earlier), students are exposed to gay Days of Silence hosted in many public schools by the Gay, Lesbian, & Straight Education Network (GLSEN).[3] They see mass same-sex "wedding" ceremonies performed in the middle of the Grammy music awards. Or how about the San Francisco public school that took a first-grade class on a field trip to a teacher's same-sex wedding?[4]

On Nickelodeon, a kids' cable network, children meet gay characters and watch same-sex kissing scenes. No, I'm not kidding. According to the Media Research Center, much of the content of Teen Nick's show *Degrassi: The Next Generation* centered around homosexual lifestyles and painted those who dissented as homophobic.[5] Now there are even calls for a lesbian Disney princess![6] Let's face it, to young evangelicals homosexuality has become a norm.

One of the greatest weapons that gay activists, the evangelical Left, and pop culture have against young evangelicals is their fear. A major reason young evangelicals will not engage and defend the church's historic teachings and views on homosexuality is the same reason they are not engaging and defending their faith in the public realm. They simply do not know enough.

The Church's Compromise

The same-sex dilemma is a prominent faith and cultural issue that young evangelicals are having to sort through without much help. In our own efforts to steer clear of tough, uncomfortable discussions, the church tends to hide from the same-sex debate. For the sake of appeasement, American Christians refuse to discuss the Bible's clearness in Christian schools, Sunday school lessons, and Sunday morning sermons. Unintentionally we led by example and taught our children how to compromise. Not only that, but many congregations are slowly and quietly embracing homosexuality as a righteous lifestyle.

Andy Stanley, son of well-respected pastor Charles Stanley, leads Georgia's North Point Community Church and, sadly, illustrates a type of quiet compromise. During a sermon in May 2012, Pastor Stanley told the story of a "modern-day" dysfunctional family in his church. The story goes that a man left his wife and child to enter into a same-sex relationship. While separated, the man and his partner asked to serve in the church. Pastor Stanley explained that he told the couple no because they were committing adultery as long as the divorce was not finalized. Pastor Stanley never addressed the evident homosexual sin in his story or his sermon.

Weeks later the *Christian Post* asked for a pointed response from Pastor Stanley on why he focused solely on the sin of adultery and did not comment on homosexuality. Pastor Stanley declined to respond, insisting only that the reporter listen to his sermon the following week. Unfortunately Pastor Stanley's next sermon dodged the homosexuality issue yet again. Just to be fair, I called North Point to ask if Pastor Stanley could offer an official statement on homosexuality and Christianity. His staff said no and referred me to his disobliging sermon series.[7]

Certainly a balance exists that cherishes compassion without compromise. Though not a cakewalk by any means, it is possible to love and minister to our gay neighbors while still upholding God's model for sexuality, marriage, and family.

It's a Tough Discussion

Before confronting the same-sex dilemma silencing Millennials, older evangelicals must first conquer their own fears. Engaging in the same-sex debate is intimidating, even for pro-family veterans. Worse is that the lesbian-gay-bisexual-transgender (LGBT) community hurls verbal attacks and fear-mongering tactics at young Christians who uphold biblical marriage. (Just google "Chelsen Vicari" and the word *gay* to see what I mean.) The pressures and threats launched on those who protect marriage are severe, but we will tackle that topic in chapter 9.

For now we will arm ourselves with knowledge of Scripture in order to speak intelligently and truthfully in a spirit of love to this intimidating issue. Together we will also wade through social science, which confirms marriage is the foundation that supports healthy families and nations.

As you read along, ask the Holy Spirit to give you understanding of the Bible's teachings and social science's findings. Ask for courage and strength to rally for marriage as God intended within your state and federal legislatures. Above all, pray for courage as you speak His truths while showing love to your neighbors in same-sex relationships.

What Does the Bible Say?

There is no "gray area" when it comes to God and the creation of male and female or sexuality. Seven passages in the Bible explicitly identify God's model for heterosexual sexuality and marriage:

- Genesis 1:27

- Genesis 2:24–25

- Leviticus 18:22

- Leviticus 20:13

- Romans 1:26–27

- 1 Corinthians 6:9

- 1 Timothy 1:10

It is important for evangelicals to keep in mind that a rejection of homosexuality does not begin with a retelling of the destruction of Sodom and Gomorrah, as is often done. It instead starts literally "in the beginning." In the very first chapter of the first book of the Bible, we see that God established complementary heterosexual sexuality:

> God created man in his own image, in the image of God he created him; male and female he created them.
>
> —GENESIS 1:27

It is not by accident that God created only one man and his biological complement, woman, to love, support, and replenish the earth. This divine intention was God's model for marriage and is highlighted a few verses on:

> Therefore a man shall leave his father and his mother and hold fast to his wife, and they shall become one flesh. And the man and his wife were both naked and were not ashamed.
>
> —GENESIS 2:24–25

According to John Stott, a respected New Testament scholar, there are three great truths about family and the same-sex debate revealed in Genesis 1 and 2: (1) the human need for companionship, (2) the divine provision to meet this need, and (3) the resulting institution of marriage.[8]

Stott, who one columnist half-joked would be evangelicals' version of the pope if ever elected, warned, "It is significant that those who are advocating same-sex partnerships usually omit Genesis 1 and 2 from their discussion, even though Jesus our Lord himself endorsed those teachings of these passages."⁹

Many among the evangelical Left are not satisfied with Genesis's establishment of sexuality and marriage, and they quickly dismiss the Old Testament model. In their revisionist view they deem the Bible badly mistranslated by mankind. Therefore we can't condemn the LGBT community with Scripture verses. But as Joe Dallas, coauthor of *The Complete Christian Guide to Understanding Homosexuality*, points out:

> There's no contingency in the Bible about homosexuality. It doesn't say, "Thou shalt not lie with man as with woman, unless that's your orientation." The biblical authors probably weren't concerned about what caused certain behaviors—they were concerned with the behaviors themselves. By the way, it's quite an insult to God and his Word to ignore what the Bible says about homosexuality just because its authors never heard of "sexual orientation."¹⁰

By dismissing the Genesis marriage model, the evangelical Left is also dismissing Jesus Christ. While teaching in Judea, Jesus affirmed God's divine establishment of marriage after He was approached by Pharisees. One rabbi asked, "Is it lawful to divorce one's wife for any cause?" Jesus pointed back to Genesis when He answered, "Have you not read that he who created them from the beginning made them male and female, and said, 'Therefore a man shall leave his father and his mother and hold fast to his wife, and the two shall become one flesh'? So they are no longer two but one flesh. What therefore God has joined together, let not man separate" (Matt. 19:3–6).

It is hardly open to debate that Jesus was not commenting simply on adultery instead of the divine institution of hetero-sexual marriage. Kenneth Erwin III, a cultural analyst who has worked within the pro-family movement for the last decade, explained:

> It is naïve and a desperate grasp at straws to argue that Jesus was only supporting one man and one woman in regards to the adultery question. Jesus was speaking to a Jewish rabbi in front of a Jewish crowd regarding sexual immorality. And the Jews' context for sexual immorality is found in Leviticus law which states plain as day that homosexuality was wrong.[11]

That moral law described in Leviticus explicitly states:

> Do not have sexual relations with a man as one does with a woman; that is detestable.
>
> —LEVITICUS 18:22, NIV

> If a man has sexual relations with a man as one does with a woman, both of them have done what is detestable. They are to be put to death; their blood will be on their own heads.
>
> —LEVITICUS 20:13, NIV

Finally, the apostle Paul supports both God's divine institution of heterosexual sexuality and marriage and Jesus's affirmation of this model by plainly addressing homosexuality as a sin in his letters to the Romans, the Corinthians, and to Timothy:

> For this reason God gave them up to dishonorable passions. For their women exchanged natural relations for those that are contrary to nature; and the men likewise gave up natural relations with women and were consumed with passion for one another, men committing shameless acts with men and receiving in themselves the due penalty for their error.
>
> —ROMANS 1:26–27

> Or do you not know that the unrighteous will not inherit
> the kingdom of God? Do not be deceived: neither the sexu-
> ally immoral, nor idolaters, nor adulterers, nor men who
> practice homosexuality, nor thieves, nor the greedy, nor
> drunkards, nor revilers, nor swindlers will inherit the
> kingdom of God.
>   —1 CORINTHIANS 6:9–10

> The sexually immoral, men who practice homosexuality,
> enslavers, liars, perjurers, and whatever else is contrary to
> sound doctrine.
>   —1 TIMOTHY 1:10

These passages may seem straightforward, but those who support homosexuality often dismiss them as "clobber verses." I
warn you that if you are having a theological discussion about
homosexuality and pull from one of the previously quoted scrip-
tures, there is good chance you will be accused of dodging a
complex issue by hiding behind one of the so-called "clobber
verses," and the theological discussion will end.

My response to those who reject the use of Scripture in the
same-sex debate is to raise this question: If we do not look to
Scripture for moral guidance, then where do we look? I think
they would agree that we certainly can't depend on our own
fallen selves to reinterpret the Bible. The good news is that even
if the person shuts down when you present Scripture, the conversation can continue by refocusing the dialogue on current social
science, which continues to support God's model for marriage
and family.

What Makes a Family?

Millennials in the church constantly want to take the stay-out-
of-it route when it comes to same-sex marriage. They find it hard
to digest that marriage must look and function in one specific
way. What they have come to believe is that marriage is whatever

an individual wants it to be. Sadly, they picked up this mentality in the church.

Christians must not look upon the same-sex marriage debate with a "holier than thou" attitude. The truth is that churches stopped engaging and defending marriage and family long before same-sex marriage became front-page news.

The church stopped defending marriage when fast-and-loose, no-fault divorces became fashionable in the church. We did so when adultery, premarital sex, and cohabitation were no longer condemned from the pulpit. We let go of the family unit when dads walked out on their families and left fifteen million US children fatherless.[12] That was when the church dropped the ball on marriage.

Since then attitudes toward marriage continue to shift in the wrong direction. A 2013 Gallup poll found that 52 percent of Americans say they would vote in favor of same-sex marriage while only 43 percent would vote against it.[13] Our refusal to publicly defend marriage as God intended is what initially led to the redefinition of marriage. This fact must cause us to ask ourselves what will become of marriage if churches remain silent, or worse, endorse homosexuality.

Maggie Gallagher, cofounder of the National Organization for Marriage, suggests marriage would disappear altogether if churches remain silent about God's plan for human sexuality and marriage. She notes:

> Marriage loses its shape and purpose by being transformed into an individual freedom. If it is just a private and personal decision the logic leads not to gay marriage, but to the abolition of marriage as a legal status.[14]

The same society that promotes the dislocation of marriage is also overlooking the effects the deconstruction of the family will have on America's children. Because kids do better with a mother and a father. They just do.

A 2012 New Families Structure Study, led by University of Texas sociologist Mark Regnerus, caused outrage among the LGBT community when the research revealed that when compared to youngsters reared in a traditional family, children raised by homosexual parents:

- Are much more likely to grow up on welfare

- Have lower grades in school

- Report less stability in their family unit

- Report ongoing "negative" impacts from their family unit

- Are more likely to suffer from depression

- Have higher arrest rates

- If female, tend to be more sexually promiscuous[15]

A second study, this time conducted in Canada, affirmed part of the findings of the New Families Structure Study: kids fare worse in school when raised by same-sex parents.[16] The social science doesn't stop there. Janice Shaw Crouse, senior research fellow for the Beverly LaHaye Institute and author of *Children at Risk*, stated:

> American children are at risk in carefully documented ways when they are raised in any household but a married mom-and-dad family: They make worse grades, are likely to drop out of school, more prone to getting into trouble, have greater health problems, are more likely to experiment with drugs and/or alcohol, and will likely engage in early sexual activity and thus be more likely to contract

a sexually transmitted disease, have an abortion(s) and/or teen pregnancy.[17]

Too often Millennials I know do not want to engage in the public fight over marriage because they think same-sex couples aren't hurting anyone else. "Leave them be," young evangelicals say. On that same falsehood, I heard a pastor say from the pulpit, "Don't worry about marriage out there. Just live out yours well." Taking a passive approach to God's marriage model is not the answer because if we do so, society will undermine its most fundamental institution.

The legitimization of same-sex marriage places the very stability of our nation at risk. The traditional family unit is the foundation upon which all successful civilizations have been built. The destruction of holy matrimony will cause a cultural avalanche.

While testifying on behalf of traditional marriage before the Maryland Senate, Mario Diaz, Esq., legal counsel for Concerned Women for America, explained:

> Our human experiences moved us *out of* practices like polygamy, homosexual "marriages," and restrictions on interracial marriages, confirming every time that God's model for marriage is best. These perceived "discriminations" or restrictions defining marriage preserve the necessary ingredients for us to continue to progress and flourish as a free society.[18]

I couldn't agree more.

Back to Basics

Young evangelicals are exposed to a dangerous lie that tells them the Bible does not condemn individuals acting on same-sex attractions. "Jesus never said homosexuality was wrong" or

"There are all kinds of families in the Bible" are just some of the arguments young evangelicals hear. But the truth is there is only black and white when it comes to God's creation of sexuality, marriage, and family.

While talking with a group of my LGBT friends, I asked them to please explain how they affirm their gay lifestyle when the Bible clearly presents the family as led by a mother and a father. One bright young man answered that the Bible is full of different types of families, including those with multiple wives, and therefore does not prescribe one father and one mother. In fact, he continued, the nuclear family unit we know today wasn't even established until the Industrial Revolution.

While my friend's heartfelt answer seems convincing, it is wholly inaccurate. The Bible does mention unconventional families. For instance, we know that King Solomon had more than a thousand wives and concubines. But we must not confuse the Bible's recording of cultural practices as biblical endorsements. We can learn from the men and women in the Bible, who found out for themselves that having multiple wives only caused strife, chaos, and dysfunction.

Remember King David's many wives and concubines? David's redefinition of marriage caused great turmoil in his family when his son Amnon became obsessed with his half-sister Tamar. Tragically Amnon raped and then rejected her. Then Tamar's full brother Absalom plotted the murder of his half-brother Amnon. What happened next isn't pretty. (See 2 Samuel 13:1–29.)

The defense of marriage as God intended, in private and public, is not born out of bigotry or fear. Instead, it is the result of a long, arduous journey mankind had to take before finding ourselves back at the model God intentionally created. Family, and consequently children and nations, function best when there is one father and one mother leading the home.

Can We Love?

Jesus's instructions were clear: "You shall love your neighbor as yourself" (Mark 12:31). Likewise, the apostle John wrote, "If someone says, 'I love God,' and hates his brother, he is a liar." He continued, "And this commandment we have from Him: that he who loves God must love his brother also" (1 John 4:20–21, NKJV).

Culture warriors and concerned Christians, we have a biblical responsibility that even outweighs the defense of marriage: love. We are to demonstrate love and kindness toward our neighbors in same-sex relationships. This is not compromise but compassion. Demonstrating unconditional love to our homosexual neighbors, however, is not easy. Beware that it requires more than just a few kind words. First, we have to tear down some really tall walls.

Going back to that discussion with my LGBT friends, I asked several of them how, or even if, Christian parents, family, and friends can maintain biblical principles on sexuality and marriage and still love those attracted to the same sex. The consensus was that the LGBT community believes conservative Christians will always have an "endgame" and will hope and pray for their transformation. So to show love, we were encouraged by some to check our convictions at the door and simply walk through life with them. This information was not very helpful or hopeful.

Leaving my convictions at the door was certainly not an option. A lightbulb finally went off when a lesbian friend of mine asked me, "How do you think God sees a homosexual?" I told her, "The exact same way He sees me. He loves us the same." My friend first registered shock, which was unsurprising because for so long LGBT activists have painted conservative Christians as hateful brutes. That individual later confessed that she was afraid to meet me after reading my pro-family work. Then after the shock faded, she expressed relief, and we were able to talk civilly about God's expectations for her life and mine.

The truth is that every one of us is called to love and serve humanity. All humanity. Not just Americans. Not just the unborn. Not just Protestants. Not just conservatives. Not just liberals. As evangelicals we deeply care about the souls of people as well as cultural stability and public safety.

We cannot ignore the outrageous suicide rate of teenagers who are attracted to the same sex. According to a study done by the Suicide Prevention Resource Center, same-sex attracted youth between the ages fifteen and twenty-four are up to seven times more likely to attempt suicide than heterosexual teens.[19]

A pastor cannot wait to decide what to say on the issue of homosexuality when he has a young man struggling with same-sex attraction staring at him asking for help. All churches should be proactive and clear on how to communicate God's model for sexuality and marriage, but we must be just as clear to communicate God's unflinching love. The church must provide a safe place for these teens. When the church offers no talks, no hugs, no assurances, no truth, and only ejection and condemnation, we cause devastating pain.

The truth is that if traditional churches responded differently when teens explained they are attracted to the same sex, we could not only show love but also provide a safe space and hope in Jesus Christ. Showing hate and rejection only causes more hurt and fear. It also causes these teens to run into the waiting arms of the LGBT community, which is literally acting as honorary moms and dads to same-sex-attracted Christians who have been excommunicated from their families.

Remember that by demonstrating God's truth with a loving spirit, we don't succumb to pride or hate. Groups such as the Westboro Baptist Church, whose picket signs read "Death Penalty 4 Fags" and "God Hates Fags," do not accurately reflect the church.[20] Their unbiblical and harsh messages wound our homosexual neighbors and keep them from discovering Christ's transforming grace. But when we are silent, this group and other extreme sides of the "fundamentalist" bandwagon are what frightened young men and woman see as the face of the church.

I'll be the first to admit that the religious Right hasn't always gotten the same-sex dilemma right either. In the past some conservatives' political strategies included demonizing same-sex attracted individuals in order to gain political ground. But thankfully this is not the overriding sentiment of the pro-family movement.

To be perfectly clear, showing love will not require a retreat from the pro-family movement or the defense of traditional marriage. Actually, the message of truth in love is growing among the pro-family sector. For instance, the new evangelical campaign Imago Dei pledges, "I recognize that every human being, in and out of the womb, carries the image of God; without exception. Therefore, I will treat everyone with love and respect."[21]

Among those who have signed the Imago Dei pledge is Focus on the Family President Jim Daly. Recently Daly told *Time* magazine, "People have said love the sinner, hate the sin. So often I think that has fallen woefully short, and it certainly appears like we are hating the sinner as well as the sin. And that is the difference—you've got to recalibrate and say I know you are made in God's image, and therefore you deserve my respect."[22]

He Calls You Beloved

The same-sex dilemma is not simply a public policy issue. It is also deeply personal. These men and women are not the labels they wear: gay, lesbian, transgender, bisexual. They are human beings. They are Americans. They are someone's son or daughter. Most of those in the LGBT community are real, broken, vulnerable, thoughtful, creative, emotional individuals struggling to navigate through this life, just like the rest of us sinners.

Your heart might be aching for your child or best friend who struggles with same-sex attraction. For you this is not just another cultural battle. It is a tug-of-war over the heart and mind of your loved one. And so you might be trying to figure out how to love and support your child or friend while still upholding biblical principles.

Popular Christian author and speaker Nancy Heche knows firsthand the heart-wrenching experience of having a beloved child tell her, "I'm gay." Nancy is the mother of actress Anne Heche, who was in a relationship with talk-show host Ellen DeGeneres during the 1990s. After an awful public spectacle, Nancy asked God what she could possibly do to help her daughter. Nancy recounts her "aha" moment:

> I could confess my own sin. And I could bless her [Anne]...to bless is to ask God to interfere, to take action in one's life to bring them to the desired relationship with Himself so that they are truly blessed and fully satisfied. When God blesses He releases His power to change the character and destiny of the one being blessed.[23]

Nancy went on to say, "Sure, there's a place for discussing things, speaking the truth in love, and putting boundaries in place when you need to. But when it's all been said and done, you still don't have the power to change another person's mind."[24]

Speaking truth in love to a gay child or neighbor is possible, but it isn't easy. Christopher Doyle is the cofounder and president of Voice of the Voiceless, an ex-gay advocacy group. Doyle is a former homosexual who grew up in a Pentecostal/charismatic church and accepted Jesus when he was five years old. When I asked him how Christian parents and the evangelical community should respond to their gay friends, loved ones, and neighbors, Doyle said:

> We need to love everyone regardless of their behavior and lifestyle choices, listen to their pain, and welcome them into our churches. However, we should not dilute the truth that: (1) no one is born with homosexual feelings; (2) no one chooses to experience homosexual feelings; and (3) change is possible. Ultimately, to adopt a "gay" identity is a choice that a person with same-sex attractions makes. Somewhere along the line, they chose to embrace a "gay" identity instead of an identity in Christ, and rather than seeking to understand the meaning of their same-sex attraction and healing the wounds that led to these feelings, they embraced and accepted that "gay" was who they are.[25]

Finally, to the young man or woman who is currently struggling with same-sex attraction, I want you to know that you are loved. It is true that in the name of Christianity some people have mistreated their gay brothers and sisters and misrepresented the love of Jesus Christ. They are wrong, and this is far from the sentiments of the conservative Christians I work alongside. We love you. In fact, there is nothing you could ever do that would make us stop loving you or remove you from the transforming love of Jesus.

Also, I want you to know that you are not alone in the church community. If you are dealing with anxiety, depression, or loneliness, please talk with someone about your feelings. There is a wealth of resources and Christian counseling and therapeutic organizations that offer help and support. Here is a list of Christ-centered resources:

- Desert Stream Ministries: 866-359-0500

- International Healing Foundation: 301-805-6111

- Homosexuals Anonymous Fellowship Services: 281-746-0172

These men and women, boys and girls, need a church who will speak truth into confusion and tell them who God says they are—that they are made in His image, loved extravagantly, and capable of turning from sin and leading a holy and virtuous life. The reality is that all of us are by nature fallen and broken and in need of redemption and forgiveness. Homosexuality is just one of many manifestations of our fallen nature. As Michael Brown, PhD, wrote in his book, *Can You Be Gay and Christian?*, "It is no harder for a homosexually oriented person to follow Jesus than it is for a heterosexually oriented person to follow Him, since He requires everything from everyone who chooses to follow Him as Lord. He said repeatedly, 'If anyone would come after me, let him deny himself and take up his cross daily and follow me' (Luke 9:23)....Jesus requires the same thing from all of us...everything."[26]

Chapter 5

UNMASKING THE
SOCIAL JUSTICE FAÇADE

> *By mixing a little truth with it, they*
> *made their lie far stronger.*[1]
>
> C. S. LEWIS

HE STEREOTYPE THAT MILLENNIALS ARE SELFISH, SPOILED, and conceited doesn't fit most young evangelicals I know. Last summer I chaperoned a youth mission trip to Hinche, Haiti. Located in the center of the country, Hinche is a tiny village of rocky clay roads, thatched-roofed homes (if you can even call them that), and scarce modern conveniences. Another female chaperone warned me to prepare for complaining teenage girls who were out of their comfort zones.

Bucket showers and ketchup spaghetti breakfasts were hard to handle, but not for whom you'd think. While some of the other chaperones and I were begging the Lord for strength to endure one more day of bug bites, the teens were joyfully planting fruit trees in the village, pouring concrete at a construction site, and asking for second helpings at meal time. And when the chaperones were jogging through the airport to ensure we didn't miss our plane home, the teens were planning their return trip. Doesn't sound very self-centered, does it?

Thanks to Facebook, Twitter, Skype, and other forms of social media, Millennials' eyes are open to the struggles around the world. They can't ignore the brokenness. Their compassion mixed with youthful naiveté makes them capable of bringing great change. But it also makes them vulnerable. Too often "social justice" is the sheepskin socialism wears to make inroads into evangelicalism.

Buzzwords such as *justice, inequality,* and *marginalized* catch their attention. So when the evangelical Left confuses the church's mission to further God's kingdom with unlimited big government and defines expanded regulatory and social welfare as "social justice," young evangelicals buy in.

Let me be clear: I am a social justice advocate. Social justice is love in action, and it is prescribed by the Almighty for Christian living. We must care about others' suffering in order to (1) love our neighbors as ourselves, (2) develop relationships and farther spread the gospel, and (3) follow the example of Jesus. As Robert George of Princeton University said, "When we are criticizing 'social justice,' we don't mean it in the honorable sense in which it has been used in our tradition. We mean it in the corrupted sense that some people, not all people, use it."[2]

The Bible doesn't mince words when it comes to our social responsibility. According to Proverbs 21:13, "Whoever closes his ear to the cry of the poor will himself call out and not be answered." It's true that the evangelical community hasn't always gotten social justice right. In an effort to right our wrongs, young evangelicals are unwittingly mistaking the gospel for socialism.

What's Wrong With Social Justice?

Shane Claiborne is a well-intentioned young Christian leader who has built a following living out social justice through The

Simple Way, his nonprofit commune in inner-city Philadelphia. For all the good he does in Philadelphia and all the good he has inspired others to do, Claiborne preaches a social justice gospel mixed with far-leftist error.

For example, Claiborne held a "jubilee" demonstration on the steps of Wall Street to confront capitalism, which he has called a "system that produces beggars."[3] Never mind the fact that capitalism has inspired innovation, empowered ordinary Americans to generate wealth, and made the United States into an economic powerhouse, Claiborne would throw the baby out with the proverbial bathwater. Although Claiborne may correctly recognize excesses and injustices committed by *some* capitalists, condemning the entire system does more to further socialist ambitions than God's kingdom.

Similarly the evangelical Left is often outspoken in its calls for peace on the world stage. The problem is that it typically blurs peace with the appeasement of ruthless regimes that oppose human rights and, at times, vilify the United States. In March 2014 IRD reported on comments liberal evangelical leader Tony Campolo made in an online podcast. In it Campolo said he "fully" understood why North Korea would not release American missionary Kenneth Bae from its deadly prisons. The reason, Campolo alleged, is that "missionaries here in the United States have been too close to the CIA."[4]

Praise God that Mr. Campolo realized how his hurtful assumptions undermined a fellow Christian simply trying to share the Word of God with North Koreans. Shortly after our report was published, Campolo's assistant phoned IRD to express Campolo's regrets for making the comment. The podcast has since been removed from Campolo's website.

Claiborne has made similar untenable statements. On the eleventh anniversary of September 11, 2001, Claiborne suggested that al Qaeda's attack on the United States that murdered nearly three thousand people was payback for the 1973 CIA-backed coup in Chile that also took place on September 11. Claiborne posted on his Facebook page:

> In 1973, the democratically elected government of Salvador Allende was overthrown in Chile by a CIA-backed coup.
>
> In 2001, terrorist attacks on the World Trade Center and the United States Pentagon killed twenty-eight hundred people.[5]

IRD president Mark Tooley responded to Claiborne's disturbing parallel, writing: "This rhetoric about the 'first 9-11' is common on the far-left, which imagines all sins originate ultimately in the U.S. and that any attack on the U.S. is predictable 'blowback.'... Their ideology also demonizes the United States as the 'empire' and source of much of the world's evil. They do not profess any interest in or concern about what would replace the United States as chief world power."[6]

I'll never forget one Memorial Day while I was still in college when I visited my parents' church. The pastor talked about how America is blessed with tremendous freedom and democracy because of our Christian foundations. I distinctly remember cringing, arms folded through the whole sermon. At the campus church I had been attending, I was learning that America's capitalist system was oppressing the poor, promoting greed, and causing conflict around the world. Thanks to a godly international politics professor, the blinders eventually came off.

Claiborne and those on the evangelical Left generally don't refer to themselves as socialists or communists. But other progressive Christians herald the same far-left political ideas and call it socialism.

Jeremiah Wright, pastor emeritus of President Barack Obama's former church, Trinity United Church of Christ in Chicago, is one such Christian. In a sermon Wright looked to social justice and liberation theology to bring a socialist utopia, where peace, justice, and righteousness reign. Wright assured his congregation that Isaiah 2:4 prophesied of "a global community where there would be peace among all mankind." He also claimed that the prophet Micah sounds a lot like a socialist.

> Micah preached in Jerusalem between 725 and 705 BC. He preached about the promised community. He preached against injustice....Now listen, neither Hannity, Beck, O'Reilly, nor the Tea Party would have liked Micah at all. When you read his work, Micah sounds like a left-wing liberal. He sounds like a liberation theologian. Plus, Micah was black. That would make him a black liberation theologian. Instead of preaching prosperity and capitalism mistakenly called Christianity, Micah sounded like a socialist. Micah almost sounds like a Marxist....Micah preached peace, not preemptive strikes. Peace, not empire theology. Peace, not a strong military presence. Peace.[7]

Wright and the confused social justice activists are making the same mistakes as the collectivists before them. They are overlooking the basic sinful nature of humanity. Collective acts by human beings will never make a perfectly peaceful world because we are sinful.

In their book *One Faith* professors Thomas Oden and J. I. Packer explained, "Some, inspired by a utopian vision, seem to suggest that God's Kingdom, in all its fullness, can be built on earth. We do not subscribe to this view, since Scripture informs us of the reality and pervasiveness of both personal and societal sin (Is. 1:10-26; Amos 2:6-8; Mic. 2:1-10; Rom 1:28-32)."[8]

Paul Alexander, copresident of the left-leaning advocacy group Evangelicals for Social Action, was recently dismissed as an Assemblies of God minister for merging social action with leftist political ideology. According to IRD's Jeffrey Walton, while addressing the Society for Pentecostal Studies Alexander endorsed same-sex marriage, used biblical Egypt as the "construct of whiteness," and "offered an unorthodox interpretation of Christ's interaction with the Canaanite woman in Matthew Chapter 15 who seeks healing for her demon possessed daughter, charging that she did not come to worship Jesus, but to challenge him."[9]

In addition Alexander said:

> The Canaanite woman's reframing of the dog-bread metaphor elicited the transformation in Jesus that he needed to escape the confines of *whiteness*. He suffered the humiliation of the Canaanite woman and learned deeper obedience to God's will.[10]

Young evangelicals follow people like Claiborne and Alexander largely because any backlash leads to claims that you are "uncompassionate" or "not following Jesus's example." These insults do not faze seasoned evangelicals and conservatives who are grounded in their faith. But for young evangelicals still trying to crack the code of theology, false claims that we are being "unjust" or "greedy" can be effective—albeit petty—tools used to silence us.

Justice Theology

Undergirding progressive Christians' social justice rhetoric is a theology that incorporates liberal, social, and economic agendas into a sweet-sounding religious paradigm. While attending my first progressive Christian conference for IRD—the Jopa Group's Christianity21 (C21) conference—I heard the term "justice theology" used in more than one breakout session. From what I've gathered, justice theology is a nod to liberation theology, only it is rebranded to attract young evangelicals and mainline Protestants.

You should know that justice theology's ancestor, liberation theology, traces its roots back to the early twentieth century within Catholic and Protestant circles. Liberation theology aimed to merge Marxism and Christianity largely in Latin America and Soviet Russia. Shedding the adjective "liberation" is a crafty strategy. Liberation connotes revolution and anarchy. "Justice," of course, is a softer-sounding term that typically evokes sympathy.

Here's how they do it: they lump in every left-wing political agenda, add the word "justice" behind it, and hope no one notices.

For example, *Sojourners* magazine's tagline is "Faith in Action for Social Justice." But in their March 2014 issue, topics revolved around Obamacare, climate change, and pacifism. The very first article after Jim Wallis's editor's note is a discussion responding to the question, "What's right about Obamacare?"[11]

Sojourners board member Carol Keehan writes, "Obstructing the effort to get health insurance and causing people to be without it because of our actions is a dangerous activity on many levels— we can't forget Jesus' words that 'whatever you do to the least of these, you do to me.' This admonition helps us realize that our work for access to health care isn't optional or trivial. It's sacred."[12] Unfortunately Keehan does not mention the federal health care mandate's infringement on Christians' religious freedom by requiring taxpayers to pay for abortion-inducing drugs.

Here's another example: Recognizing how pro-life young evangelicals are, progressive Christian blogger Benjamin Corey wrote an article titled "10 Things You Can't Do and Still Call Yourself 'Pro-Life.'" In it Corey cleverly tried to convince his young audience that those who are truly pro-life support liberal social and economic policies. To call yourself pro-life, Corey writes, you cannot:

- Oppose health care for all
- Support unrestricted gun rights

- Advocate, support, or passively tolerate economic policies that oppress the poor, minorities, or any other marginalized group

- Oppose gender equality

- Support the death penalty

- Oppose increasing the minimum wage

- Support, advocate for, or participate in war

- Use dehumanizing language such as "illegal"

- Cannot hold anti-immigrant sentiments or support oppressive immigration policies

- Support unrestricted, elective abortions after the age of viability[13]

I'm glad Corey includes that last item, but if you're anything like me, such a list might leave you scratching your head. Judging from this list, "good" evangelicals who care about one biblical social issue must also endorse government health care mandates, federal infringements on religious liberty, and gun control, and disapprove of our military men and women's sacrificial efforts to preserve our freedoms. These liberal political ends are obviously not what it means to be "pro-life." But as soon as a friend of mine posted Corey's blog on Facebook, several of my Christian acquaintances from college agreed with *all* of Corey's points.

That is why it's so important our evangelical parents and leaders—the "grown-ups" in the room—demonstrate how to effect social change in accordance with Scripture. One evangelical offering such leadership is Pastor Jerry Falwell Jr., president of Liberty University. Falwell understands the difference between Christian outreach and government overreach. He explained, "Jesus taught that we should give to the poor and support widows, but he never said that we should elect a government that would take money from our neighbor's hand and give it to the poor.... If we all did as Jesus did when he helped the poor, we wouldn't need the government."[14]

You likely have enough experience to know that the church, never the government, is best equipped to effect change for the common good. If a single mom needs help paying her bills or buying her kids groceries, the church should assist her financially. Food pantries should be a part of every local church's outreach plan, and fortunately many churches recognize this. Beverly LaHaye, founder of Concerned Women for America, writes: "I know of churches where single mothers are helped by members who baby-sit for them, prepare and deliver meals, pray with them, give financial gifts, drive them to church on Sunday, and assist in many other ways. Many churches have support groups for single moms. This is love in action."[15]

Christians are generous, compassionate people. In fact, conservative Christians have proven themselves more generous and "compassionate" than their liberal neighbors. According to a 2006 ABC News report, research showed that conservatives donate 30 percent more to charities than do liberals. Oh, and the best, most encouraging part is that conservative families donated even though they made slightly less money than liberal families.[16]

Rejecting dependency on an expanded government isn't uncompassionate. I'll give you one of my favorite commonsense examples: Let's say I have a friend who is dependent on alcohol. He constantly asks me for vodka. In an effort to show him compassion, I buy his vodka every week. But one day a stranger tells me I shouldn't buy my friend's vodka anymore because it was only causing my friend more harm. Would you call that stranger uncompassionate? No. You would, however, call me a bad friend for constantly supplying vodka to an alcoholic!

The Social Justice Jesus on College Campuses

There is a long-held impression among evangelical parents that by sending their children to evangelical colleges, they create a safe haven away from distorted teachings and biased political agendas. Unfortunately this impression is a false sense of security. Evangelical campuses may be the very place they are introduced to the social justice Jesus.

The college classroom environment can be especially daunting for conservative evangelical students. Trust me. It stunk to speak up in my political science classes and call for cuts in government entitlements. Liberal students refuted all my points by claiming I *obviously* did not care about the poor, the sick, the elderly, or the helpless. How could I respond? This was the turning point that made social justice Jesus so appealing to me.

What is worse is when these same arguments are pitched at Christian colleges by Christ-professing faculty and staff. Just as leftist thought is coddled in the ivory towers of secular and mainline Protestant universities and seminaries, so too is the altar of tolerance being erected within evangelical academia. Over coffee I asked a friend with a background in Christian higher education to which evangelical colleges he would feel comfortable sending his children. My friend could think of only a few, and, sadly, most of them are not well-known.

Curious about the state of evangelical academia, I started asking questions. While visiting Southwestern Baptist Theological Seminary, I went to dinner in downtown Fort Worth, Texas, with a group of students. On the drive we passed Texas Christian University (TCU). I asked my hosts if they had considered attending this particular school. They shook their heads no and explained it wasn't as "Christian" as it once was. Not entirely sure what that meant nor wanting to rely on hearsay, I started doing some digging.

I searched the school's website and could not find a statement of faith. Its vague mission statement was absent of any mention of Jesus Christ or Christ-centered education. It did mention a connection with the Christian Church (Disciples of Christ), a denomination with a "passion for justice."[17]

More digging produced a TCU blog titled "How Christian Is Texas Christian University?" Written by a school admissions counselor, the blog dodges the question raised by discussing how the "Constitutionally-protected separation between church and state prevents Christianity from being the 'official' American religion." If you're wondering what this has to do with the university, well, the admission counselor explains, "TCU, as an institution, is not quite like America, but it's also not completely dissimilar." But to ease any parents' fear that their children are not getting a solid Christian education, TCU does "require students to take one religiously-themed class."[18]

Declining Christian teachings on evangelical campuses is not an isolated occurrence. In 2010 Azusa Pacific University (APU) gathered dozens of faculty from evangelical campuses around the country for its third annual Christians on Diversity in the Academy conference. Speakers hailed from Biola University, Geneva College, George Fox University, Covenant College, Redeemer University College, Simpson University, and Missouri Baptist University. Sadly, justice theology, though they did not refer to it by name, was smeared throughout the sessions.

The theme of the conference was "Thinking Critically for the New Decade." Sounds harmless enough—that is, until you peek beyond the surface. Social justice buzzwords paired with liberal politics swarmed. One session was titled "White, Male, and Middle Class: Assessing the Future of Liberation Theologies From a Position of Privilege." Another was "'Then Jesus Rebuked Them': Reflections on Privilege, Power and Prejudice in Luke 9:51-10:12."[19]

Faculty from George Fox University presented a paper that attempted to establish parallels "between the oppression of the ancient Hebrews, the South Africans during Apartheid, and minorities in our current society." The presenter concluded his abstract with a quote from Malcom X, a proponent of violence during the civil rights movement.[20] Perhaps the presenter missed English class the day his professor reviewed irony.

Unfortunately the justice/liberation theology didn't end there. Most infuriating was a presentation by APU's own staff member, Shaynah Neshama, titled "The Evolving Doctrine of Gender Equality." Praise for same-sex marriage, abortion, abortifacients, and controversial contraception was woven into the synopsis, which stated:

> Twentieth century marked unprecedented achievements in women's human rights. The spectrum of advancements arrays from greater awareness of violence against women to *equality in marriage* and *reproductive rights* to educational and employment rights.[21]

Eric Teetsel, executive director of the Manhattan Declaration, was a graduate student at APU for a short time. He withdrew from his program after an invited guest speaker advocating same-sex marriage rebuked him for referring to Scripture's affirmation of marriage between one man and one woman. According to Teetsel, this incident was merely the last straw after a host of similar incidents while at APU.

But it wasn't just at APU. During an interview, Teetsel told me that while working in higher education at Colorado Christian University, he would attend the annual Association for Christians in Student Development conference. While in one of the sessions, Teetsel vividly remembers an anti-Israel guest speaker talking fondly of Iran. Teetsel told me: "This was right around the time that Ahmadinejad had written a letter published in the

Washington Post and Bush ignored it essentially, because you don't write letters back and forth to dictators. This Christian speaking to all of these higher-ed administrators—thousands of them—was talking about how Ahmadinejad was an example of morality, love, and respectful dialogue of differences. And President Bush was the one who failed to live up to respectful [discourse]."[22]

There is good news. Sacrificing traditional Christian teaching for the sake of "diversity" doesn't necessarily lead to a booming university. The Institute on Religion and Public Life's publication *First Things*, following *USA Today*'s rubric for "Best Colleges," crafted its own rankings among Christian universities.

Wheaton College stole the top spot for most seriously Protestant university, and the King's College in Manhattan was deemed a school "on the rise, filled with excitement." APU, however, was ranked next to last in the list of Christians schools "on the decline and filled with gloom."[23]

The Future According to Justice Theology

Back at the C21 conference, the justice "theologians" endeavored to answer one big question: What must we do to ensure Christianity's vibrant, lasting future?

Laced throughout almost every presentation was one common thread: the future of Christianity depends on reaching out to those marginalized by their sexual orientation, race, gender, class, and culture. Telling, perhaps, was that there was no mention of reaching the next generation of young people.

To demonstrate the diversity rubric for saving Christianity, Ani Zonneveld, a female imam and founder of Muslims for Progressive Values, was invited to offer her take on the future of religion and social justice. The "emergent Muslim" asserted that the marginalized should be at the center of not only Christianity but also any religion that hopes to thrive in America in the coming years.

Moving away from the traditional platitudes of Islam, Zonneveld's paradigm shift focused on:

1. Freedom of speech

2. Universal human rights

3. Women's rights

4. LGBTQ rights

5. Critical analysis and interpretation

6. Compassion

7. Diversity[24]

To promote this agenda within Christianity, C21 speaker Enuma Okoror, author of *Reluctant Pilgrim*, claimed that "America has to acknowledge and grapple with the ways in which its unique form of Christianity must be a tad more wrapped up in culture than in faith."[25]

In the words of my mother, "Never lose your compassion, but don't let go of your conviction either." Make no mistake: abandoning core tenets of the faith in the name of social justice is a sure plan for disaster.

A brighter future for Christianity's social witness starts with transformation through the saving grace of Jesus Christ; pursuing truth in Scripture; and caring for the orphan, the widow, and the sex-trafficking victim while behaving morally in accordance with the Word of God. Our goal should never be to let go of the truth in order to reach out to others; it should be to seek prudential justice through a healthy civil society based on law and liberty for all.

When our church youth returned from the Haiti mission

trip I described at the beginning of this chapter, the kids had an enormous passion to aid everyone in need. So the youth used our food pantry as an outlet to channel their zeal for outreach. It would have been a shame if the church had not found a way to channel the kids' enthusiasm. Calls for the church's self-examination are not completely unwarranted. It's true that too many youth groups return home from missions trips and do nothing more until the next mission trip. When it comes to caring for our neighbors, Millennials are ready to learn. But the church must be willing to lead.

Chapter 6

UNVEILING THE JESUS FEMINISTS

> *The fact that I am a woman does not make me a different kind of Christian, but the fact that I am a Christian makes me a different kind of woman.*[1]
>
> ELISABETH ELLIOT

N ITS SEPTEMBER 2012 ISSUE *VOGUE* MAGAZINE ASKED former University of Florida quarterback Tim Tebow what qualities he hopes to find in his future wife. An outspoken evangelical, the then-twenty-five-year-old Tebow replied, "Being attracted to someone plays a big part, but there's also so much more than that for me. It's about finding someone sweet and kind—and that has a servant's heart."[2] Unsurprisingly his remarks were met by a media backlash.

A popular feminist blog spot dubbed Jezebel (seriously, that's their chosen name) misinterpreted Tebow's statement and accused him of searching out a woman who is merely "hot, kind, and servile."[3] Thankfully, another evangelical man came to Tebow's defense. Russell Moore, PhD, president of the Southern

Baptist Convention's Ethics & Religious Liberty Commission, clarified why Tebow was not a male chauvinist jock.

In his blog, *Moore to the Point*, Dr. Moore explained that within Christianity, "Husbands serve wives. Wives serve husbands. Children serve parents. Parents serve children. Pastors serve churches. Churches serve pastors. That concept might be demeaning in the world of *Vogue*, but it's not in a new creation where 'the leader is the one who serves' (Lk. 22:26)."[4]

Amen, Dr. Moore! Too bad this understanding is so hard for many to grasp. On August 11, 2011, in Ames, Iowa, a poised and confident Rep. Michele Bachmann stood at her podium next to seven equally self-assured male opponents during her very first Republican presidential debate. No doubt she was expecting just about anything—except, perhaps, the curveball she was about to be thrown.

Addressing the only female presidential candidate, conservative *Washington Examiner* columnist Byron York asked, "As president would you be submissive to your husband?" York's question was met with boos from the audience. As for Rep. Bachmann, she just smiled and answered, "What submission means to us—if that's what your question is—it means respect. I respect my husband. He's a wonderful, godly man and a great father, and he respects me as his wife. That's how we operate our marriage."[5]

Rep. Bachmann's unapologetic explanation of submission in a Christian marriage didn't faze the Iowa audience, and she won the Iowa straw poll. The mainstream media, however, went into a tailspin.

A perplexed Chris Matthews, host of MSNBC's *Hardball*, told his guests, "I grew up with…old-fashioned parents. I understand, to an extent, the 'who's the boss' thing and…'father knows best' stuff from the fifties. But would she let her husband tell her who to vote for, for example? I mean where does this thing end, this husband is the power boss?"[6] Acknowledging that Rep. Bachmann speaks a lingo that other evangelical Christians understand, Matthews mocked, "Are they riding across the West in a wagon train, these people? Where do they live?"[7]

Phrases such as "submissive wife," "servant's heart," and "biblical womanhood" are understandably puzzling terms to secular society. For that reason they typically spark strong reactions from the feminist elite who have worked tirelessly to raise a generation of Millennials who accept modern feminism as the norm.

Yet, increasingly, those terms are being met with equal ire from evangelicals who have swallowed the leftist hype that equates submission with female oppression. A biblical view of womanhood teaches nothing of the sort. The problem is, the evangelical Left has traded in a true, biblical view of womanhood for a repackaged version of feminism, and that is the message they are feeding Millennials.

Home Sweet Home

Make no mistake: feminism is not dead. According to Phyllis Schlafly, a longtime pro-life activist, lawyer, and mother of six, "While people associate feminism within the 1960s revolution, since that is when feminism began, feminism and feminists didn't disappear just because they're no longer marching in the streets. They simply chucked the loud protests and morphed into the fabric of society."[8]

Indeed, from the ivory towers of academia, feminist elites soundlessly passed their sociopolitical torch to impressionable college students, including me. Unless one embraced feminism, it would have been virtually impossible to graduate with honors from my liberal arts university. My papers were not graded based upon my writing and researching skills. They were judged by the ideology in my arguments. I learned quickly that espousing feminism was a college woman's ticket to the dean's list.

Still, no matter how hard I tried, the feminist mantras never quite meshed with my Christian beliefs. I found myself constantly qualifying my views. "I'm a feminist…but the government should not provide abortions—that's murder." "I'm a feminist…but I submit to the authority of the Bible." "I'm a feminist…but I'm not a victim." Finally I realized I wasn't a feminist at all.

Upon graduating, I figured I would be leaving the leftist feminist ideology behind. I was wrong. Feminists are not content to remain within their cozy campus offices. Modern feminists—who scoff at belief systems purporting that God made male and female with separate, complementary roles—have, ironically, moved to a new home: the church.

By blurring the lines between the values-centered women's rights movement of the nineteenth century and the women's liberation movement of the sixties, some women within the new Christian left are presenting a new spin on feminist liberation ideology that goes way beyond bra burning and hairy legs. Depending on the Jesus feminist you talk with, prerogatives can range anywhere from dismissing the unique roles between women and men to heralding a contraception mentality that views unplanned children as a problem in need of a solution, therefore requiring taxpayer-funded contraception, abortifacients, and at times, abortion.

The feminist views widely accepted in liberal colleges are starting to emit from evangelical churches, schools, and seminaries as female leaders attempt to convince Millennials that one can be both a feminist and a Christian. What's worse, perhaps, is that Millennials are buying it. Pat Ennis, EdD, the distinguished professor of homemaking at Southwestern Baptist Theological Seminary, told me that her students—pastors' wives and young women raised in Baptist churches (not the typical evangelical Left crowd)—are eagerly sympathizing with feminist ideas. The evangelical community has become like the proverbial frog dropped in a pot of water that is being heated slowly, Dr. Ennis explained. "We don't even realize in the evangelical community…that we have been cooked and the feminist movement has moved in."[9]

A Jesus Fem—What?

In January 2013, *New York* magazine's Alissa Quart reported in her article "I Am a Feminist Because Jesus Made Me One" that feminism is increasingly influencing today's Christian culture in a trend being called "Jesus feminism."[10] In her book *Jesus Feminist* author Sarah Bessey offers her definition of a feminist: "At the core, feminism simply consists of the radical notion that women are people, too. Feminism only means we champion the dignity, rights, responsibilities and glories of women as equal in importance—not greater than, but certainly not less than—to those of men, and we refuse discrimination against women."[11]

Sound harmless? Who wouldn't support championing the dignity, rights, and glories of women as equal in importance to that of men? Bessey is right when she says "patriarchy is not God's dream for humanity."[12] Who wouldn't object to discrimination against women? The problem with Bessey's argument is that she cites feminism as the solution to patriarchy and inexcusable cases of sexism within some churches. She then claims it is time to "revisit and reimagine" God's role for women. Sadly, some men have used the Bible to harm women, but that is not an accurate representation of the gospel nor a good reason to challenge God's equally valued but distinct characteristics and roles for women.

Popular among young evangelicals especially, the Jesus feminists are trying to "liberate" women from their supposed "oppressed" place in the church and home. In Bessey's book she broadly portrays conservative Christians as having an agenda that sees women as inferior to men.[13] Bessey appears more gracious than many among the Christian Left, but it is unfair that she offers her readers a vague, misleading understanding of traditional Christian teaching. Obviously, as an unmarried woman without children who works outside the home, I would not subscribe to a view that declares women should be barefoot, pregnant, and in the kitchen. That would be absurd!

It is even more absurd to herald feminism as the means to free women from a presumed place of bondage within conservative churches. These claims of "liberation" are all too familiar to the pro-life, pro-family culture warriors who have faced off with feminists for years in an attempt to put an end to the slaughter of unborn life and women's sexual exploitation.

Bessey would like us to think feminism is a victim of misguided stereotypes. She writes, "I know feminism carries a lot of baggage, particularly within the evangelical church. There are the stereotypes: shrill killjoys, man-haters, and rabid abortion-pushers, extreme lesbians…deriding motherhood and homemaking."[14] I'm sorry, but this is not simply "fearmongering misinformation," as Bessey puts it.[15] These characteristics are *exactly* what feminism looks like.

Let me be perfectly clear: I am not a theologian. Nor do I find it necessary in this book to present a litany of hermeneutical arguments about gender roles. I'll save those discussions for the Bible scholars. What I am is a public policy analyst and professional pro-life, pro-family advocate who knows that terms such as "gender equality" are nice-sounding phrases, but they offer no real redemption.

Actually, feminism has oftentimes proven to victimize women further instead of seeing us for what we are: fearless, hardworking, gracious, smart, nurturing—the list goes on. Have you heard of the so-called "war on women"? It is a slogan feminists use to rally support for taxpayer-funded contraception. By doing this, feminists portray women as single-issues voters, concerned only with free birth control. But women are smarter than that. We are concerned about job growth, fiscal responsibility in Congress, national security, raising families, feeding the hungry, and sharing the gospel. The "war on women" is what feminists concocted to set themselves up as a type of gallant savior for presumed weak and helpless women. Well, thank you very much, but women already have a Savior. He looks nothing like a feminist.

What a "Jesus Feminist" Looks Like

Attempting to reconcile evangelical values with feminism is dangerous. Still, the evangelical Left keeps trying. Laura Turner, daughter of prominent evangelical pastor John Ortberg, is one such figure who conveniently ignores the troubling ideology behind much of today's feminism and declares, "Feminism is simply the belief that women are equally as human as men— equal in the eyes of God, equal in image-bearing, equal in ability. (This is why it is possible to be both a feminist and a complementarian...)."[16]

Obviously, the Christian faith has no problem with this view of women. But Turner goes on to quote from Sarah Bessey's book, "Christian feminists can celebrate any sort of feminism that brings more justice and human flourishing to the world."[17] Oh, *if only* feminism were that innocent. That would make my job of defending life, the welfare of women, and family *so* much easier.

Warning: Feminism is *not* so simple. So let's put the word into perspective. According to Candi Finch, assistant professor of "feminist theology" at Southwestern Baptist Theological Seminary, feminism is defined in two unconnected ways:

- *Feminism is a movement*—a social, historical movement seeking rights for women; an organized activity on behalf of women's rights and interests.

- *Feminism is a philosophy or ideology*—the theory of political, economic, and social equality of the sexes.[18]

Despite how sweet the evangelical Left tries to make it sound, Jesus feminism is a closer reflection of modern-day feminism than the righteous, nineteenth-century movement that centered around the abolition of slavery, discrimination, and voter rights. Christian women are certainly people too. As a single, working, twentysomething woman, I'll be the first to advocate for our respect and basic human rights. But as Christian apologist Ravi Zacharias aptly put it, "We cannot talk about human rights without the right to be human."[19]

Jesus feminists are leading the evangelical Left's so-called "family planning" crusade. But let's get real. We all know that includes abortion. Calling herself a "femmevangelical," Jennifer Crumpton admits that her goals include abortion access. An outspoken feminist mouthpiece for the evangelical Left and a contributor to *A New Evangelical Manifesto*, Crumpton writes in her Patheos blog:

> For over half the population—and potential workforce and brain-trust—of our country, our right to control our own bodies and *make decisions about our own reproductive systems is an economic issue.* Our right to freely access our choice of *no-cost contraception* without the knowledge, moral judgment or consent of our bosses is an *economic issue.* Our right to *family planning,* to decide when and if we will have children, with whom, how many children we will have and the spacing of them is an *economic issue. Our right to affordable health care* that does not charge women up to 48% higher premiums than men or penalize female status (sometimes even including past experience of rape or domestic violence) as a "pre-existing condition," is an *economic issue.*[20]

Crumpton, like many others, suggests that abortion has become an unfortunate necessity. "Listen, everyone agrees that life is precious and sacred, and no one *wants* abortions," she writes. "But life is extraordinarily complex and often very unfair to women, especially poor women, on many levels."[21] While such arguments may sound compassionate, they actually make women into victims, which is hardly empowering.

Yet this talking point is one of them most commonly used among the evangelical Left, as popular blogger Rachel Held Evans (who wrote the foreword for Bessey's book) illustrates. In a blog titled "Privilege and the Pill" (because the blame always comes back around to an elusive, rich white American man), Evans makes her case for taxpayer-funded contraception, including abortifacents: "Abortions happen because of unwanted pregnancies, and often, unwanted pregnancies happen because of lack of contraception. Most women who choose to have abortions do so because they feel they cannot manage the financial burden of carrying out the pregnancy and raising another child."[22]

Unhindered access to contraception even if it comes at the expense of religious liberty? Really? That's a God-honoring solution to unintended pregnancy? So far, the Jesus feminist rhetoric doesn't overtly champion a pro-abortion mind-set, but neither do feminists who denounce women's "restrictive role of...kitchen, church, and children."[23]

Crumpton's "no-cost contraception" and "our own reproductive systems is an economic issue" rhetoric is eerily similar to that of 1950s French feminist philosopher Simone de Beauvoir, whose book *The Second Sex* appeared in America in 1953. De Beauvoir was a socialist who argued that the government had a responsibility to provide contraception and abortion to level the playing field for women. De Beauvoir said:

> A world where men and women would be equal is easy to
> visualize, for that precisely is what the Soviet Revolution

> *promised*: women raised and trained exactly like men
> were to work under the same conditions and for the same
> wages...marriage was to be based on a free agreement that
> the spouses could break at will; maternity was to be vol-
> untary, which meant that contraception and abortion be
> authorized and that, on the other hand, all mothers and
> their children were to have exactly the same rights, in or
> out of marriage; pregnancy leaves paid for by the State,
> which would assume charge of children.[24]

Did you notice how de Beauvoir's nice-sounding promises
come at a high price? Sure, Soviet women would gain maternity
leave and on-demand contraception and even abortion, but they
first had to trade their parental rights to the government, which
would "assume charge of children."

Similarly, some of the Jesus feminists' intentions are sweet-
sounding, but no one is stopping to think deeply enough about
the costs. In America are Christian women willing to trade in
our precious religious liberty for the sake of taxpayer-funded
contraception, abortifacients, and abortion? Are we really ready
to make that trade? For the sake of our children and future
grandchildren, I pray not.

When longtime feminist advocate Gloria Steinem was asked
what the greatest threat facing women today was, her response
encapsulated the views of many Jesus feminists. She answered,
"Female bodies are still the battleground, whether that means
restricting freedom, birth control and safe abortion in order
to turn them into factories, or abandoning female infants
because females are less valuable for everything other than
reproduction."[25]

Jesus feminists sound an awful lot like Steinem, which is a
shame, because as Christians we of all people should know
that we don't have to devalue the unborn in order to empower
women. Many of the nineteenth-century suffragists and

abolitionists understood that. They cherished family values and spoke out against the evils of abortion. "Family planning" was certainly never endorsed by heroic suffragists such as Alice Paul and Elizabeth Cady Stanton. Alice Paul, the original author of the Equal Rights Amendment, said, "Abortion is the ultimate exploitation of women."[26] Similarly, Elizabeth Cady Stanton said, "When we consider that women are treated as property, it is degrading to women that we should treat our children as property to be disposed of as we see fit."[27]

Calls for contraception may seem harmless enough, and in truth the concerns companies such as Hobby Lobby have expressed are over abortion-inducing contraceptives, not all birth control. But it is worth pointing out that the pill did not exactly set women free. Sure, when it works properly, the pill enables couples to determine when to begin their families. But the pill helped birth the sexual revolution, which altered society's moral standards by removing pregnancy as a natural result of promiscuity.

This, ironically, made it easier for money-hungry businessmen to objectify women's once-cherished sexuality, as Mary Eberstadt explained in her book *Adam and Eve After the Pill*.[28] Soon our photo-shopped bodies were plastered on the front pages of *Cosmopolitan* and *Hustler*, and pornography became a $10 billion industry,[29] emergency contraception became a sex trafficker's best friend, and out the door went men's accountability.

As with all drugs, the pill comes with health risks. Recently ABC News reported that one hundred fifty women filed complaints against Essure birth control. One woman described her reaction to the drug, saying, "Every time I would sit down, I would feel like something was poking my stomach. I would feel horrible, horrible pain."[30] Additionally the National Cancer Institute acknowledged the pill increases women's chances of developing breast, cervical, and liver cancer.[31] YAZ, one of the most popular oral contraceptives used by women, has a long list of harmful side effects, including gallbladder disease, headache, mood changes, and irregular vaginal bleeding.[32] Before evangelicals blindly shove oral and chemical contraception into women's hands as a means of preventing abortion, we need to be honest with ourselves and others about the potential health risks.

Warping Biblical Principles

Tell any secular feminist that you are thankful God blessed you with ovaries so you can have the privilege of bearing children, and see what happens. Modern feminists such as Jessica Valenti will likely remind you that, "Whether it's [reproductive] rights, violence against women, or just plain old vanilla sexism, most issues affecting women...exist to keep women 'in their place.'"[33] Within religious communities, they argue, patriarchal white men use God and His authority to keep women "in their place."

Even if well-intentioned, Jesus feminists too often chip away at the authority of Scripture to realize their vision of gender equality. They diminish the truth that God created men and women equal but distinct, and by doing so they risk robbing women of their dignity, integrity, uniqueness, and the special responsibilities entrusted to them by God.

Janice Shaw Crouse, director and senior fellow of the Beverly LaHaye Institute, a faith-based women's public policy think tank, explained to me, "There is a huge difference...between the biblical principle of equality—by which God created all of us as equal—and the...radical feminist principles that push hatred of masculine traits and try to get rid of the differences between women and men."[34]

In hopes of establishing gender equality, the Jesus feminists have commandeered Galatians 3:28, which reads, "There is neither Jew nor Greek, there is neither slave nor free, there is no male and female, for you are all one in Christ Jesus." But in its context this verse is describing the level spiritual standing all who believe in Christ have, not disqualifying our uniqueness as separate yet complementary reflections of the image of God.

At Q's Women and Calling conference held in November 2103, I listened as Rachel Held Evans told a room full of Christian women that the Bible doesn't provide women with a guideline by which to live our lives. Evans said:

> Here's the thing. I have searched high and low. I've combed through commentary after commentary. I spent a year of my life immersed in this idea of biblical womanhood, and I never found a blueprint for how to be a woman of faith.... The Bible doesn't give us a blueprint. God doesn't communicate to us in bullet points. Instead God uses poetry, history, letters...and mostly stories to communicate with us. And stories don't make great blueprints, do they?

Kathy Keller addressed Evans's misleading critique of biblical womanhood in a pointed review of *A Year of Biblical Womanhood*. Noting that Evans chose to live by the Old Testament Levitical code rather than the commands the Bible "*genuinely* addresses to Christian women," Keller challenges Evans for "ignoring (actually, by pretending you did not know about) the most basic rules of hermeneutics and biblical interpretation that have been agreed upon for centuries"—namely, "that Jesus' coming made the Old Testament sacrificial system and ceremonial laws obsolete."[35]

Keller continued, "You...proclaimed at the start of your book: 'From the Old Testament to the New Testament, from Genesis to Revelation, from the Levitical code to the letters of Paul, there [will be] *no picking and choosing*' (xvii, emphasis mine). To insist that it would be 'picking and choosing' to preclude the Levitical code from your practice of biblical womanhood is disingenuous, if not outright deceptive."[36]

There is no need for women to cherry-pick which parts of Scripture we trust. Granted, there are men who have selfishly twisted Scripture in order to abuse and mistreat women. But these men are wrong. Acknowledging that there are differences between men and women does not prevent women from becoming stellar lawyers, writers, mothers, and wives. God's Word does not oppress women and place them below some glass ceiling. It does the complete opposite! Within traditional Christian teaching, women are raised up, loved, and revered:

> Husbands, love your wives, just as Christ loved the church and gave himself up for her to make her holy, cleansing her by the washing with water through the word, and to present her to himself as a radiant church, without stain or wrinkle or any other blemish, but holy and blameless. In this same way, husbands ought to love their wives as their own bodies. He who loves his wife loves himself.
> —EPHESIANS 5:25–28, NIV

Ephesians makes no mention of slavery, oppression, or patriarchal ownership. On the other hand, feminists' efforts have placed women under a microscope and have led to much anxiety, insecurity, and a life of striving to "have it all."

Feminism Enslaves Women

Feminists know their version of womanhood is unhealthy. That's why feminist elites don't follow their own formula. *Cosmopolitan* editor in chief and feminist icon Helen Gurley Brown told women that "if you're not a sex object, you're in trouble" and encouraged them to reject marriage and enjoy multiple sexual partners.[37] But this lifestyle only leaves women feeling used and ultimately alone—which is probably why Gurley Brown did not take her own advice! She opted instead for a stable, faithful, fifty-one-year marriage that lasted until her husband, David Brown, died in 2010.[38]

Feminism is only happy with *choice* when that choice does not include family, children, and homemaking. Don't take my word for it. Just ask Rebecca Walker, daughter of notorious feminist Alice Walker, author of *The Color Purple*. Rebecca admits that as a child she "yearned for a traditional mother" because her own mother believed that "children enslave women" and eventually disowned her daughter.[39]

Rebecca wrote:

> When I hit my 20s...I could feel my biological clock ticking, but I felt if I listened to it, I would be betraying my mother and all she had taught me.... In fact, having a child has been the most rewarding experience of my life.... My only regret is that I discovered the joys of motherhood so late—I have been trying for a second child, but so far with no luck.
>
> Feminism has betrayed an entire generation of women into childlessness.... But far from taking responsibility for this, the leaders of the women's movement close ranks against anyone who dares to question them—as I have learned to my cost.... I believe feminism is an experiment, and all experiments need to be assessed on their results. Then, when you see huge mistakes have been paid, you need to make alterations.[40]

It is feminism that holds women captive. We are not free to choose for ourselves but are forced to accept a liberal political and socioeconomic laundry list of values. If women fail to accept this, they are marginalized and mocked. They tell us evangelicals are riding the "wagon train," as Chris Matthews put it, and that we will never be smart or sophisticated enough if we dissent.

Jesus feminists continue to cite male leadership as suppressive to evangelical women. Granted, there have been cases where men have twisted Scripture to abuse and hurt women. Those men were wrong, and their actions are inexcusable. But the Bible does not endorse gender discrimination.

Why do feminists challenge a woman's role in the home rather than giving us the freedom to follow our own path? Feminist forerunner Simone de Beauvoir offers a clue. "No woman should be authorized to stay at home to raise her children," de Beauvoir told her protégé Betty Friedan. "Women should not have that choice, precisely because if there is such a choice, too many women will make that one."[41]

Feminism has placed a stigma on motherhood, subtly (and not-so-subtly) suggesting that women who choose homemaking and motherhood are not as accomplished as those working outside the home. Worse, they marginalize and mock any woman who does not fall in line. This is not freedom; it's plain intolerance, discrimination, and oppression.

In secular society and, sadly, the church, young women are taught that feminism is their freedom. Let us never forget that God is *the* ultimate source of female empowerment, who offers us value far beyond equality. He offers dignity, purpose, hope, and everlasting life. If that isn't freedom, then what is?

Fortunately the feminist message is being countered. At the first-ever The Art of Homemaking Conference: Making Your House a Home, conservative evangelical women called for a renewed respect for women who choose to be stay-at-home mothers. During a plenary session Dorothy Patterson, a Southwestern Baptist Theological Seminary professor and wife of seminary president Paige Patterson, acknowledged:

> I am, without apology, family-obsessed....I love Southwestern Seminary. I love being able to do all the things that I'm gifted to do in some measure....But nothing outside our home is more important than the home....I just wanted you to know that you're doing the

most important thing on God's earth, the most important thing in molding the next generation.... When you get to heaven I hope you're going to join me at the throne because I'm going to look forward to sharing some crowns with the Lord Jesus, crowns that come from the work He's given me to do, which the world doesn't think is important. But I'm here to tell you the Lord Jesus thinks it's important.... You keep on keeping on.... Go home and keep on keeping on.[42]

Feminism Diminishes God's Value of Women

It's disturbing to learn that a study found 82 percent of women would prefer to pay for their own dinner on a first date than expect the man to prove he can provide for them.[43] But this trend is indicative of feminism's impact on culture. Society no longer expects men to love and respect women enough to put them on a pedestal.

Sadly, it seems, women have been taught that they can count only on themselves, and if they want to be successful and fulfilled in life, they must don power suits and act like men. As a case in point, in her best-selling book *Lean In: Women, Work, and the Will to Lead*, Facebook COO Sheryl Sandberg encourages women to adopt shrewd, dominant behavior if they want to compete with their male counterparts. It is only then, according to Sandberg, that women will attain measurable success.

While some of her advice is helpful for young women, Sandberg's complaint is that too many "highly trained women are scaling back and dropping out of the workforce in high numbers" in order to become stay-at-home wives and mothers. Sandberg then quotes Judith Rodin, the first woman to serve as president of an Ivy League university and president of the Rockefeller Foundation, who said, "My generation fought so hard to give all of you choices. We believe in choices. But choosing to leave the workforce was not the choice we thought so many of you would make."[44]

Here's the reality: evangelical women are neither victims nor enslaved. I'm sure the women behind the Jesus feminist movement are well-intentioned and have a deep love and concern for their sisters in Christ. But attempting to promote contraception, abortion, and socialism, and distorting and demeaning traditional women's ministry in the name of Christ is not the way to show concern for women.

Christianity tells women we are unique and deserving of special treatment just because we are children of God. We, like all believers, find our identity in Christ. Christian women do not have to compete with anyone. When we seek God first and don't strive to find fulfillment in the things we do, whether our work is inside or outside the home, we find His peace, wisdom, and providence, and truly "have it all."

Not a Feminist—a Jesus Follower

Instead of embracing feminist goals, let's look to the evangelical women of the 1960s and 1970s who spoke out against an ideology that conflicted with their theology.[45] Unlike the women within today's evangelical Left, female leaders during the women's liberation movement refused to embrace the current trend.

There are Christian women today still bucking the popular trends. Recognizing that the premier feminist activist group, the National Organization for Women (NOW), did not reflect her convictions or those of any of the Christian women she knew, Beverly LaHaye, wife of evangelical pastor and author Tim LaHaye, took action. "We were determined to stand in opposition to them," she wrote in *Who But a Woman?* "But we knew we had to do more than simply oppose feminism; we knew we must actively promote pro-family values in America."[46]

LaHaye displayed her strength as a concerned Christian

woman and started her own organization, Concerned Women for America (CWA). Not one to be saddled by her so-called "oppressed" state in the home and church, LaHaye formed CWA with a small group of women around her kitchen table. "No longer do feminists have a monopoly," she wrote. "No longer can they claim to speak for all American women. We are here, hundreds of thousands now, telling the world that feminism is a false view of the world."[47]

Today CWA has five hundred thousand members spanning almost all fifty states, and it is America's largest public policy women's organization.[48] Meanwhile, NOW seems to have adopted same-sex activism in order to maintain its relevance. In the end, advocating on behalf of women simply as a Christian, and not as a feminist, paid off.

Women—Baptist, Pentecostal, charismatic, nondenominational, or what have you—are certainly people too. We are trailblazers. But we do not pave the way for ourselves but for Jesus Christ.

The truth is, we accept and are fulfilled by a purpose feminists dare not recognize. Christian women are already liberated not by ideology or a worldly status but by Jesus Christ. "For freedom Christ has set us free; stand firm therefore, and do not submit again to a yoke of slavery" (Gal. 5:1).

Unlike feminists, we do not have to prove our worth, our skills, or our smarts to the world. As Christians, our purpose is much greater. Our liberation, our career callings, our sheer hope are found in Jesus Christ. Those who recognize that truth are not called Jesus feminists. They're called Jesus followers.

Chapter 7

DEFENDING EVERY LIFE

I've noticed that everybody that is for abortion has already been born.[1]

RONALD REAGAN

F THERE IS EVER A CONTEST FOR THE BEST KID-FRIENDLY, pro-life resource on the market, Dr. Seuss's *Horton Hears a Who!* should be a top contender. My Sunday school kids *love* it. The story entails heroism, friendship, loyalty, and best of all, a call to defend those too helpless to defend themselves, just as Proverbs 31:8–9 instructs.

In this tale Horton the elephant hears a faint scream for help coming from a pellet-sized dust ball. On that small speck, tiny Whos are housed in their city of Whoville. When Horton agrees to protect the Whos from a deadly fate, a feisty mama kangaroo tells everyone that he is crazy. Mocked and marginalized, Horton stands by his promise to shield his newfound friends by urging, "Even though you can't see them, or hear them at all, a person's a person, no matter how small."[2]

Brimming with pro-life sentiments, the story's rhythmic lines assert that despite society's standards every life deserves dignity and preservation. The funny thing is, the story's author, Theodor

Seuss Geisel, was not a pro-life advocate. To my knowledge he wasn't known to be a Christian or a conservative, but he did not have to wear either of those labels to write a pro-life message. Defending human life "no matter how small" is not a political or religious issue. The sanctity of life is written on our hearts.

In the all-time best-selling Book, the psalmist penned:

> For You formed my inward parts; You covered me in my mother's womb. I will praise You, for I am fearfully and wonderfully made; marvelous are Your works, and that my soul knows very well. My frame was not hidden from You, when I was made in secret, and skillfully wrought in the lowest parts of the earth. Your eyes saw my substance, being yet unformed. And in Your book they all were written, the days fashioned for me, when as yet there were none of them.
>
> —Psalm 139:13–16, NKJV

Tragically, American society is far removed from both Horton's proclamation and the beautiful affirmation of unborn life in Psalms. But the truth still remains that whether we are fully formed, still being formed, or imperfectly formed, each one of us was shaped by the Creator with no hierarchy of value placed on our lives.

Doesn't it bring tears to your eyes to read that even while in utero, our "soul knows very well" our Creator? Likewise, it sends shivers up my spine to think about how God knew the soul of every precious boy and girl among the 55,772,015 babies victimized by abortion.[3] For some progressive Christians, and many secular citizens, the soul of the unborn is not the most significant criteria for measuring the value of a life. Of more importance, it seems, are whether a parent has adequate material possessions, whether having children is convenient, and whether a child is wanted.

As US Congressman Henry Hyde put it so well, "This is…a debate about our understanding of human dignity, what it means

to be a member of the human family, even though tiny, power-less and unwanted."[4] It's time to end the slaughter.

Unapologetically Abortion "Obsessed"

"Unfathomable" and "heart-wrenching" are the only words I can think of to describe the horrific destruction of unborn babies and the harmful impact abortion has had on women since 1973. It was then that the US Supreme Court heard arguments for life and for death in *Roe v. Wade*. Death won big-time.

Abortion is legalized genocide. So there is no eloquent way to write that nearly four thousand unborn babies are killed every day in the United States through abortion.[5] That is why we keep fighting for life.

It's no secret that conservative evangelicals fervently celebrate unborn life. We do so because the tagline "a person's a person" is woven throughout the gospel narrative and overshadows other well-intentioned discussion surrounding poverty, injustice, and climate change.

For these reasons I'm always struck by the criticisms hurled by the evangelical Left accusing conservative evangelicals of obsessing over abortion and acting as single-issue voters[6]—as if that's always a bad thing. If we deny the God-given right to live on this earth, then how much can the ozone layer really matter?

Unlike the bandwagon following the progressive Left, conser-vative evangelicals don't care if being pro-life is cool or the policy issue *du jour*. We keep fighting because as Dr. Mildred Jefferson, the first African American woman to graduate from Harvard Medical School, said, "The fight for the right to life is not the cause of a special few, but the cause of every man, woman and child who cares not only about his or her own family, but the whole family of man."[7]

The good news is we are being heard. Americans' views on abortion are almost at a dead heat, with 47 percent describing themselves as pro-choice and 46 percent calling themselves pro-life.[8] According to a recent Gallup poll, roughly 70 percent of Americans are in favor of limiting or banning abortion. Gallup found that 21 percent of respondents believe abortion should be illegal in all cases while 50 percent think it should be legal "only under certain circumstances."[9]

That's not all. After Philadelphia abortionist Kermit Gosnell's "house of horrors" abortion clinic showed the ugly face of abortion in the form of baby feet in jars, infanticide, and the death of a mother, Americans rallied behind increased abortion regulations to ensure health and safety standards at the state level, including in Kansas, North Dakota, Arkansas, and Alabama.[10]

And it's not just the "grown-ups" who are pro-life! According to a 2003 Gallup survey, a majority of teens believe abortion is morally wrong.[11] No, wait! Don't wave the victory flag yet and skip ahead to the next chapter. A May 2014 Gallup poll found that 50 percent of those eighteen to thirty-four years old are pro-choice compared to 40 percent who are pro-life.[12]

The evangelical church still has work to do when it comes to Millennials and abortion. On January 22, 2014, IRD staff and I joined hundreds of thousands of Americans on the icy, snow-laden streets of Washington DC to remember the lives lost to legalized murder. As we looked around, it was clear that the crowd of twentysomethings and teens were overwhelmingly from Catholic universities and high schools. Not enough young evangelicals stepped out of their comfort zones to march for life alongside their dedicated Catholic peers.

Thank the Lord that Millennials recognize abortion's deadly reality. But we must encourage them to get off the couch and into the public debate on this issue too. It is only when the church is "obsessively" walking up and down the halls of Congress, state capitol buildings, and abortion clinic sidewalks proclaiming the

God-given, inalienable sanctity of innocent human life that we will abolish abortion in this generation.

Planned Parenthood

Don't let the anti-life activists fool you. Abortion is a lucrative business, not a compassionate service. In 2012 America's abortion giant Planned Parenthood raked in $542 million of your hard-earned taxpayer dollars.[13] With your money they performed 327,000 abortions.[14] The Susan B. Anthony List, a national pro-life organization, published an analysis of Planned Parenthood's annual report, which revealed abortion accounted for 93 percent of their supposed "family-planning" services. Meanwhile, adoption referrals accounted for only 0.6 percent of their total services.[15]

None of these facts support Planned Parenthood's singsong about making abortion "safe, legal, and rare." But if you understand the origins of Planned Parenthood, then you'll understand what kind of bigoted business is being run.

In 1922 Margaret Sanger founded Planned Parenthood to regulate the birth of minorities, or what she called "benign imbeciles, who encourage the defective and diseased elements of humanity in their reckless and irresponsible swarming and spawning."[16] Today 79 percent of current Planned Parenthood clinics are located near African American or Hispanic/Latino communities.[17] Is that an accident?

Unfortunately, Sanger's scheme is succeeding. During 2012 more black babies were aborted than were *born* in New York City, according to the state's vital statistics. Some 31,328 black babies were aborted while only 24,758 were born. The statistical breakdown also shows that of the 73,815 abortions in the city, 42 percent of those babies were black and 31 percent were Hispanic.[18] That is a chilling and unfathomable reality.

It's infuriating that the mainstream media refuse to

acknowledge race-targeting abortion practices. Thankfully there is a dedicated pro-life movement growing within the black community. Among those speaking out is Alveda King, the niece of Martin Luther King Jr. In her op-ed "Can Blacks Survive If We Murder Our Children?" Alveda King told of her own abortion experience and poignantly wrote:

> Like my Uncle Martin, I too have a dream. I still have a dream that someday the men and women of our nation, the boys and girls of America will come to our senses, humble ourselves before God Almighty and receive His healing grace. I pray that this is the day and the hour of our deliverance. I pray that we will regain a covenant of life and finally obtain the promised liberty, justice and pursuit of happiness for all.[19]

Don't dismiss Planned Parenthood's racial discrimination as a thing of the past. Posing as a racist donor, James O'Keefe, a citizen journalist and president of Project Veritas, showcased Planned Parenthood's willingness to eliminate black babies in a mock call to a local clinic:

> **O'Keefe:** "When I underwrite an abortion, does that apply to minorities too?"
> **Planned Parenthood:** "If you specifically want to underwrite it for a minority person, you can target it that way. You can specify that that's how you want it spent."
> **O'Keefe:** "OK, yeah, because there's definitely way too many black people in Ohio. So, I'm just trying to do my part."
> **Planned Parenthood:** "Hmm. OK, whatever."
> **O'Keefe:** "Blacks especially need abortions too. So, that's what I'm trying to do."

Planned Parenthood: "Well, for whatever reason, we'll accept the money."[20]

Young evangelicals are passionate about defeating racism and classism. Exposing Planned Parenthood's history of lies will revitalize a culture war that has been painted as dated by the Left. Even more importantly, your willingness to equip Millennials with truth will spark a brand-new generation of abolitionists who will preserve the lives of America's most vulnerable.

The Contraception Myth

By now it shouldn't surprise you that the evangelical Left has political aims. The abortion arena is no different. This time it is an attempt to back the Affordable Care Act's (aka Obamacare) employer mandate, which requires faith-based institutions, charities, and business owners to violate their religious beliefs and pay for controversial contraception.

Sidestepping the contentious public abortion debates, Jonathan Merritt, Richard Cizik, Rachel Held Evans, and a whole host of others on the evangelical Left assert the myth that the way to end abortion is by passing out taxpayer-funded contraception like it's candy.[21]

Nice try, but the research and data are against them yet again. Planned Parenthood's own think tank, the Guttmacher Institute, surveyed more than ten thousand women who had abortions during 2000 and 2001. The study found that a mere 12 percent of the women cited limited access to birth control as the reason for their pregnancies and subsequent abortions.[22]

Another study was conducted by the Centers for Disease Control and Prevention (CDC) to better gauge the reasons for teenage pregnancies. To do this, the CDC surveyed teen girls aged fourteen to nineteen with unintended pregnancies. Only 13 percent reported having trouble obtaining birth control.[23]

It's not just an American problem either. Researchers in Spain analyzed the use of contraception and abortion rates between 1997 and 2007. What they found was astonishing. During that decade access and use of contraception increased to 80 percent, yet abortion also increased—by a whopping 108 percent.[24] Essentially greater access to contraception led to a false sense of security. When contraception failed, as often happens, the baby was aborted.

It makes little sense for the Left to blame the abortion rate on the high cost of birth control. Abortion is not free. Far from it! One abortion at Planned Parenthood costs between $300 and $950.[25] After an expectant mother's first trimester, abortion is even more expensive. Yet birth control in the form of condoms are free at any Planned Parenthood clinic. And Walmart, Target, Sam's Club, and Kroger pharmacies all sell contraception at nine dollars for a month's supply.[26]

Obviously a disconnect lies here that isn't solved by trumping religious freedom and providing contraception that has dangerous spiritual, mental, and physical effects on women (as we addressed in the last chapter). Once again, the logic doesn't make much sense.

Reproductive Injustice

When talks turn to how abortion hurts women, you can be sure fingers belonging to those championing so-called "reproductive justice" will robotically point at pro-life activists. They claim that women should be able to control their own bodies. They argue especially for women of color to be empowered to control their own "reproductive destiny." That, of course, means having access to abortion. To deny that, they say, is unjust.

Their compassionate-sounding rhetoric often leads pro-life Millennials to steer clear of public pro-life discourse. But the accusations hurled at pro-life advocates are false. We are not out to hurt or subjugate women. The truth is quite the opposite. But in an effort to keep the abortion business going, anti-life activists purposefully misrepresent an entire movement whose mission includes preventing post-abortion suffering.

One of the biggest misconceptions about abortions is that they are "safe." In reality they are deadly. Pro-life activists refuse to sweep under the rug the long list of women who have died as a result of botched abortions. One of the latest botched abortion victims was Jennifer Morbelli, a beautiful twenty-nine-year-old kindergarten teacher from White Plains, New York. Guided by the false claims that abortions are "safe," the expectant mother chose to end her thirty-three-week pregnancy at LeRoy Carhart's late-term abortion facility in Germantown, Maryland.[27] Operation Rescue reported that Morbelli chose to undergo the third-trimester abortion, despite the extremely dangerous risks, after learning her child had so-called "fetal anomalies."[28]

Abortionists use frightening claims of "fetal anomalies," which oftentimes refers to Down syndrome, a cleft palate, or another disability, to drive women to abort. For Morbelli, the decision cost her and her baby their lives.

Besides death, serious medical problems occur after abortion. One female physician, Elizabeth Shadigian, MD, covered these risks in her article "Reviewing the Evidence, Breaking the Silence." Dr. Shadigian wrote that abortions can lead to increased risk of breast cancer, ectopic pregnancies (a potentially life-threatening condition in which the baby grows outside the uterus), hemorrhaging, placenta previa (in which the placenta grows in the lowest part of the uterus and covers all or part of the opening to the cervix), sexual dysfunction, and pre-term birth.[29]

Abortion also takes a toll on a woman's emotional health. Anxiety, severe remorse, distress, heartache, psychological trauma that leads to hospitalization, broken relationships, self-punishment, and suicide are often reported in post-abortive women.[30] Suicide poses such a threat to post-abortive women that states such as South Dakota are implementing "suicide advisory" laws. The new measures require abortionists to tell women of the long-hidden risk before undergoing an abortion.[31]

I'll never forget a podcast interview I produced with a post-abortive woman named Jody Duffy. A former US Army officer, Jody opened up about the traumatic date rape that led to her pregnancy. With a duty to fulfill, Jody felt she could not have a baby at that time, so she had an abortion. Although she healed well physically, guilt drove her into a time of darkness and depression. "I went on with my life and tried to move on, but it started eating away at me," Jody said. "I had a very hard time concentrating after that abortion. I wasn't able to focus on what I was doing. I wasn't able to concentrate on my job. I was isolating myself. I was getting depressed. I was having anxiety."[32]

Hope was not lost for Jody. Placing her faith in Jesus Christ, she found forgiveness, healing, and hope. She joined the Silent No More pro-life campaign that raises awareness of the emotional, physical, and spiritual harms of abortion. When asked what advice she would share with post-abortive women, Jody replied, "There is hope after abortion. The message I want to get through is that you are not out there alone."[33]

Amid their accusations that pro-life advocates are "uncompassionate," anti-life activists also overlook the four thousand pro-life ministries committed to caring for women, their unborn babies, and their health. In the United States alone there are more than twenty-five hundred Crisis Pregnancy Centers (CPS).[34] These pro-life ministries offer free sonograms, pregnancy tests, parenting classes, STD testing, and counseling for post-abortion recovery.

Run largely by volunteers, the pro-life group YoungLives offers ongoing support, resources, and counseling to young women facing unintended pregnancies. These private programs—meaning they receive *zero* federal dollars—supply everything from diapers to bottles for scared and/or disadvantaged pregnant teenagers and women who would otherwise view abortion as their only option.

For many women abortion does not provide a "fix." Instead, it creates serious problems. Hiding the threats abortion poses on women's "reproductive health" is not justice. It's fraudulent and deadly. Enough is enough. The pro-life movement strives to educate women on the horrific consequence abortion can have on both themselves and their babies. That's why the pro-life cause is pro-woman.

The Heartbreaking Cases

Abortion activists will point to the "hard" cases—when a pregnancy is the result of rape, incest, or a tragic medical complication—to justify the more than *1.2 million* abortions performed each year.[35] But it is important to remember that the number of these situations pales in comparison to the number of abortions performed each year. So let's get the facts straight right up front:

- Rape and incest account for *1.5 percent* of abortions.[36]

- Medical complications account for *12 percent* of abortions.[37]

According to John Ensor and Scott Klusendorf, pro-life activists and coauthors of *Stand for Life*, it never fails that during a Q&A discussion about abortion, a young person will raise his hand and say, "OK, say a woman is raped. If she gives birth, the child will remind her of the rape—forever! Do you think abortion is wrong in that case?"[38]

Ryan Bomberger has a very unique answer to this tough

question. Ryan's biological mother was raped, but instead of abortion she chose to carry her baby to term. After his birth Ryan was adopted by loving parents who saw him as a gift from God, not a reminder of rape. Ryan and his wife, Bethany, now dedicate their lives to addressing the massive impact abortion has on the black community through their pro-life nonprofit, the Radiance Foundation.[39]

While interviewing Ryan for *World* magazine, Marvin Olasky asked, "When you hear politicians say, 'I'm opposed to abortion except in cases of rape,' do you grit your teeth?" Ryan graciously answered:

> I don't, because most of them have never talked to someone who was born as a result of rape, and they don't realize what they're saying. Some will point to that exception simply because it's convenient.... It's easy when it's just rhetoric and statistics, but when you have real flesh and blood before you and someone with a story like mine, it transforms hearts.[40]

Down-Syndrome Blessings

The total number of abortions due to "medical complications" is often inflated by cases in which prenatal tests show the baby had some kind of disability, often a cleft lip or Down syndrome. An infamous article by the *New York Times*, of all outlets, acknowledged that 90 percent of all American women who receive diagnoses of Down syndrome abort their unborn babies.[41] But as the 10 percent of parents who choose life will tell you, what initially seems like an insurmountable complication turns into a bouncing, bubbly blessing.

Lori Scheck, daughter of Tim and Beverly LaHaye, is one such mother who faced that crossroads. But she chose life. The mother of Stephen, a smart and precious boy with Down syndrome, writes:

Abortion takes the glass and heaves it over the side of a cliff while the pieces shatter on the rocks below. While it may eliminate the disappointment, sorrow and frustration, it also eliminates the hope, joy and pride of accomplishment that child can bring. What a travesty. What arrogance. What right do we have to destroy that little person because he doesn't measure up to someone's standard? If the choice were left up to the child, I am confident he or she would choose life. I know my son would.[42]

The United States is making headway in elevating individuals with Down syndrome and their families. Today many adults with Down syndrome hold jobs, pay taxes, participate in sports, fall in love, go to college, and serve as volunteers in their communities.

In March 2014 national news outlets told the story of an inspiring young man with Down syndrome whose restaurant offered "breakfast, lunch and hugs" to every customer.[43] His name is Tim Harris, and he doesn't lead a normal life—he leads an exemplary one that we could all take lessons from. Two years after Tim graduated from Eastern New Mexico University with certificates in food service and office skills, he and his parents started their restaurant "Tim's Place," where the bright entrepreneur offers patrons a meal and a loving hug.[44]

Tim is exceptional, but he is not the exception. Here are several facts about Down syndrome doctors don't always tell you:

- In the United States more than 350,000 people have Down syndrome.

- Since the 1980s, the life expectancy for people with Down syndrome has more than doubled, from twenty-three to fifty-five years of age or older.

- Children with Down syndrome are first and foremost children. They are more like other children than they are different.

- Most people with Down syndrome have some level of cognitive delay, but there is a wide spectrum of mental abilities.

- Families with a child with Down syndrome have a lower rate of divorce.

- Many siblings of children with Down syndrome have an increased awareness of special needs and develop a compassionate and caring outlook.[45]

There is more great news. There are roughly two hundred families registered with the National Down Syndrome Adoption Network at any given time. These are families who are praying to adopt a child with Down syndrome.[46]

Adoption Saves Lives

While competing in the Winter 2014 Paralympics, Jessica Long was followed by an NBC film crew. Jessica had been adopted from Russia when she was one year old and was going to reconnect face-to-face with her birth mother. When the film crew asked Jessica what she would say to her birth mother, she replied, "When I first see my Russian family, I want them to know—I want them to know that I'm not angry, that I'm not upset that they gave me up for adoption. I think that was really brave.... And I want, I want to tell her that when I see her, you know, if anything, that I have so much love for her, my mom, because she gave me life."[47]

Choosing life is just the first step. Seeing the birth of the unborn is just a starting point. Evangelicals must continue defending innocent life after those babies take their first breaths. According to James 1:27, "Religion that is pure and undefiled before God, the Father, is this: to visit orphans and widows in their affliction, and to keep oneself unstained from the world." We must do more than give lip service about the sanctity of life and the need to defend it. For the woman with the unintended pregnancy, defending life means carrying the child to term and then, perhaps, placing the baby up for adoption. But for others it means adopting, loving, and caring for that child or being there for the woman who chooses life and decides to keep her baby.

My friend and fellow young evangelical culture warrior Chelsea Patterson knows firsthand how adoption creates pro-life hearts and minds. Placed for adoption in Romania after a nineteen-year-old unwed woman realized she could not care for her baby, Chelsea was adopted by evangelical parents from North Carolina. Now twenty-three years old, Chelsea passionately promotes the sanctity of life and the demonstration of God's love through adoption.

In an article for the Southern Baptist Convention's Ethics & Religious Liberty Commission titled "Adoption: The Period to the Pro-Life Sentence," Chelsea wrote, "Without an adequate discussion on adoption, the pro-life conversation is merely a fragment instead of a complete sentence."[48] Adoption is more than a trendy issue to rally behind, as Chelsea's life story points out. It is about action.

According to the Christian Alliance for Orphans, there are 153 million children worldwide wishing and praying to be adopted by a mother and father. Adoption along with providing temporary foster care is inconvenient, costly, and selfless. It requires putting an innocent child's life and needs above our own. But isn't that what the pro-life rally call is all about? America's evangelicals need to put the pro-life issue into perspective and welcome orphans into their nuclear families. If adoption is not a possibility, then we must support those families who are trying to adopt, as the process can be long, arduous, and expensive. We all can find a way to help put the period at the end of the pro-life conversation.

Euthanasia

When you or a young evangelical think of euthanasia, you probably picture a sterile hospital environment and an elderly person who has lived a full life and is ready to die. But this is only a small aspect of much larger, more gruesome life-denying practice.

Internationally euthanasia takes many forms, including the murder of those unable to make a life-or-death "decision" for themselves. Babies born with birth defects are often the victims of euthanasia, in what is known as after-birth abortions or infanticide.

Efforts to legalize child euthanasia are under way in Belgium right now, and they have the audacity to call them "mercy killings"! To spare you the gruesome details, I will tell you only that in February 2014 Belgium's Senate voted fifty to seventeen to allow children of all ages who are terminally ill to be euthanized.[49]

In light of Belgium's movement toward legalized child euthanasia, human rights activist David Alton told the *National Catholic Register*, "You begin by saying you will only ever authorize lethal injections on a tiny number of terminally ill patients and end up with laws that take the lives of thousands with, and then without, their consent."[50]

Don't think the United States is far removed from horrific endeavors to destroy viable life. While no one has called for so-called "unwanted" children to be euthanized, listening to MSNBC anchor Melissa Harris-Perry left me shaking my head as she observed that a baby's value depends on the parents' feelings, not viability or human dignity. On air Harris-Perry said, "When does life begin? I submit the answer depends an awful lot on the feeling of the parents. A powerful feeling—but not science. The problem is that many of our policy makers want to base sweeping laws on those feelings."[51] Thank goodness a person's value doesn't really depend on feelings. But it's frightening to think anyone would think it does.

Changing Hearts and Minds

There is hope after abortion. No amount of remorse, emptiness, and pain is out of God's reach. Examples of God's incredible, restorative healing in the hearts and lives of post-abortive women are plentiful. But perhaps the most impactful account of freedom and transformation after abortion centers around a man. Dr. Bernard Nathanson was an American abortionist who admitted to presiding over more than sixty thousand abortions, one of which his own baby girl or boy.[52]

When it came to rallying behind the legalization of abortion, Dr. Nathanson was a key player. He helped establish the pro-abortion lobby group the National Association for the Repeal of Abortion Laws (NARAL), which still functions today under the name NARAL Pro-Choice America. As a lobbyist for the pro-abortion movement, he would lie about the safety of abortion in order to change public opinion.

Very little care did he give to the sanctity of unborn life until an ultrasound showed an unborn baby wriggle away from a surgical instrument and open his mouth as the tool moved closer. Dr. Nathanson could no longer deny that abortion was the intentional destruction of a precious human life. He refused to perform abortions, confessed that he lied, and became an outspoken pro-life activist.

After hearing what he called "the silent scream" of unborn babies, Dr. Nathanson gradually began to appreciate the value and dignity Christianity places on human life. This appreciation eventually led to his salvation. Dr. Nathanson was baptized in St. Patrick's Cathedral in 1996, and he committed his life to pro-life advocacy until his death in 2011. God took a past marred by sixty thousand abortions and turned it into good, proving that no one is ever too far gone.

Remember that we serve the same God who used a man who persecuted Christians to witness to the early church. If the apostle Paul wasn't out of reach, then who is? The apostle Paul wrote, "There is therefore now no condemnation for those who are in Christ Jesus. For the law of the Spirit of life has set you free in Christ Jesus from the law of sin and death" (Rom. 8:1–2). There is always hope, no matter what has happened, because in God's eyes "a person's a person."

Chapter 8

OPPOSING CHRISTIAN PERSECUTION

> *Timid men ... prefer the*
> *calm of despotism to the*
> *boisterous sea of liberty.*[1]
> THOMAS JEFFERSON

As you've probably heard, a tug-of-war between Christian convictions and government control is under way in the United States. In many countries this struggle is literally a battle to the death. While some observers think Christians are making much ado about nothing, the crux of the religious liberty dilemma is this: if American Christians don't speak out against the subtle infringements on freedom, matters will only get worse—so much so that one day there may not be much difference between religious liberty here and in nations that aggressively oppose Christianity.

No other biblical issue finds itself at the intersection of culture and faith as does religious freedom. When a Christian doctor or nurse is fired for refusing to perform an abortion, it is a religious liberty issue. When a Christian adoption agency is forced to close its doors because it seeks to place children with a mother and a father and not two fathers or two mothers, this is a religious liberty issue. When a Christian chaplain is forced to resign for praying in Jesus's name, religious liberty is at stake. To say a battle for religious liberty is raging in America is not an overstatement; it is just a matter of fact.

No, American Christians are not being harassed, tortured, or murdered the way believers in Africa, North Korea, and the Middle East are. But that doesn't make our challenges any less urgent. Although the news reports tend to center around whether Christian businesses should be forced to fund abortifacients or provide goods for same-sex commitment ceremonies, the real issue facing US believers is whether the government gets to dictate what is acceptable for Christians to think and do.

Make no mistake, the efforts to muzzle Christians are very real. It would be so much easier to advance moral relativism in the name of tolerance and secularism if Christians would stop carrying on about biblical morality and absolute truth—if we'd just bake the gay wedding cake, pass out the Plan B, and quit complaining about violations of conscience. Unfortunately for liberals, that's just not what salt and light does. It doesn't blend in. (More on that in chapter 10.)

If Christians don't speak up, a few national leaders will decide the convictions of every one of us. Evangelicals need to wake up and realize that in "the land of the free," Christianity is already being imprisoned within our sanctuaries. Sure, we can still worship God, but we'd better not do so in a way that offends anyone else—or we will be punished. We are told to keep our faith out of the streets and away from the schoolhouses. What's worse is that some of Christianity's prison guards are, in fact, professing followers of Christ.

America's Religious Climate

Before softening his article in order to publish it on Religion News Service, Tom Ehrich opened an op-ed with these scathing words, "Bigots are claiming their 'religious freedom' requires free rein for bigotry."[2] The rhetoric is familiar, but what might surprise you is that Ehrich is an active Episcopal priest who consults churches to help them become more effective in ministry.

Popular culture is growing increasingly hostile to Christians' public witness. Around the world Christians are being killed, tortured, raped, pillaged, and harassed in ways we can't even imagine. In America we aren't there yet, but that is the path we will follow if Christians continue to surrender our freedom of religion in bite-size increments.

False claims that religious persecution is just a ploy to rally über-conservative Tea Party patriots are causing young evangelicals to discount the serious consequences of inaction. Young evangelicals are not seeing this First Amendment issue for what it is—a matter that affects everyone's ability to hold to their own belief system—because pundits on the religious Left are using misrepresentations of Jesus to convince them there is no credible threat to religious liberty.

I can think of no better example of this clever leftist persuasion than when Kansas and Arizona in February 2014 attempted to pass religious liberty amendments via House Bill 2453 and Senate Bill 1062, respectively. The bills would have protected Christians from being forced to violate their consciences by providing services for same-sex commitment ceremonies. But the media attention and activist pressure were so intense even Arizona governor Jan Brewer, a Republican, vetoed the amendment.

It's interesting that eleven attorneys from different political and religious backgrounds wrote a letter to Governor Brewer explaining that the media, activists, and academia got it wrong when it came to the Arizona amendment. The amendment was not "antigay" legislation; rather, it contained "antireligious discrimination" language that would protect individuals—whether they are Christian, Muslim, Jewish, or atheist—from violating their convictions or facing lawsuits for upholding those convictions.[3] By vetoing the bill, Governor Brewer left Arizonans defenseless against violations of conscience.

The evangelical Left weighed in on the "wedding cake" debate too. Ignoring the policy implications, political commentator Kirsten Powers made waves by suggesting that Jesus Himself wouldn't rally behind the antireligious discrimination amendments. In a *USA Today* article Powers wrote, "Maybe they should just ask themselves, 'What would Jesus do?' I think he'd bake the cake."[4]

To drive home her point, Powers interviewed Andy Stanley, pastor of America's second-largest church. Stanley, who we already know refused to take a stance on the morality of homosexuality in a sermon series, told Powers that he finds it "offensive that Christians would leverage faith to support the Kansas law." He went on to say, "Serving people we don't see eye to eye with is the essence of Christianity. Jesus died for a world with which he didn't see eye to eye."[5]

So that we don't get bogged down in the ill-advised logic, let's put our understanding of Jesus back into clear view. As Jesus went about teaching the good news, He constantly called for repentance. As Concerned Women for America attorney Mario Diaz wrote in response to Powers's op-ed, "[Kirsten] confuses ministering to sinners with encouraging sinners in their sinfulness. The point of Christ's miracles (and His service) was salvation."[6]

The Gospel Coalition's Joe Carter pointed out other problems with Powers's representation of Jesus: "While it's likely Jesus sat down to eat with sinners, there's no evidence he ever rose from a table with anyone remaining unrepentant. It's possible, even likely, that some who ate with Jesus (such as during the feeding of the 5,000) left as unrepentant sinners. But, if so, it was not for lack of effort on the part of Jesus."[7]

Jesus didn't come to appease the world but to save it and

challenge His followers to sin no more. This is our daily struggle, and we don't get to cherry-pick how we follow Him.

Before He went into itinerant ministry, Jesus provided a service as a carpenter. What if a same-sex couple came to Jesus and requested that He construct their *chuppah*, a Jewish wedding canopy? Building the canopy knowing its sacred symbolism would require Jesus to contribute to the same-sex wedding celebration. What would Jesus do here? I think Jesus would not build the *chuppah*.

What we know with certainty is that Jesus would have taken the opportunity to teach about forgiveness of sins, transformation, and eternal hope. Maybe we should start doing a better job of following His example. While kindly declining business opportunities, let's share the gospel. It seems, however, that Pastor Stanley may have qualms about this. During his *USA Today* interview with Kirsten Powers he said, "If a bakery doesn't want to sell its products to a gay couple, it's their business. Literally. But leave Jesus out of it."[8]

Though Pastor Stanley might not go so far as to discourage people from sharing the gospel at their workplaces, "leaving Jesus out" of certain decisions while letting Him guide others is the exact formula that creates couch-potato, cafeteria-style Christianity. "Leaving Jesus out of it" forgoes the Great Commission by trading in the offensive aspects of the gospel for society's acceptance. It is much more comfortable to avoid controversy and be liked, so when highly influential spiritual leaders like Stanley say, "Leave Jesus out of it," of course young evangelicals are going to heed this poor advice.

Perhaps this is why Rebecca Harper, a twenty-five-year-old evangelical, told Buzzfeed Politics that social justice issues such as human trafficking are far more deserving of Millennials' attention than same-sex marriage. "I would absolutely say modern-slavery is more important than the marriage issue. It's a difference between the most basic of freedoms and something that often feels petty," Harper said. "When the marriage issue is debated on the public scene, regardless of your theological beliefs surrounding the issue, it doesn't carry the same urgency as modern-day slavery."[9]

What is missing from Harper's view is an understanding that religious freedom is precisely what allows Christians to combat evils like the human slave trade. When God is removed from society, something takes His place—and that something is not peace, justice, or unity. The void is filled with family breakdown, instability, poor leadership, abuse, and immortality—all of which contribute to social problems such as human trafficking.

Every generation has had to work to guard religious freedom. It is always at risk. The problem now is that Millennials are unaware that a break exists in the foundation holding everything good in place.

The Subtle Encroachments

It would seem that Founding Father James Madison was looking into the future when he delivered this perceptive warning: "I believe there are more instances of the abridgement of the freedom of people by gradual and silent encroachments of those in power, than by violent and sudden usurpations."[10] What a prescient summary of the current climate toward religious freedom in America.

Christian photographers, bakers, colleges, and charities are being punished for their views—despite the fact that the very first amendment to the Constitution guarantees that "Congress shall make no law respecting an establishment of religion, or prohibiting the free exercise thereof."

Christians are even being discriminated against in our military. At the US Air Force Academy in 2005 John Weida, a born-again Christian and commandant of cadets, was transferred and effectively removed from command for referencing Christ in prayers and speeches.[11] More recently a Pennsylvania Army Reserve unit referred to conservative evangelicals as potential enemies of the US government. Fox News's Todd Starnes reported that "a U.S. Army training instructor listed Evangelical Christianity and Catholicism as examples of religious extremism along with Al Qaeda and Hamas." So-called "Islamophobia" also made the instructor's list.[12]

In 2008 then-Virginia governor Tim Kaine's administration forbade public prayer "in Jesus's name." This blatant discrimination against evangelical Christians ultimately cost five Virginia state police chaplains their jobs.[13]

In August 2012 Chick-fil-A CEO Dan Cathy merely mentioned his personal—not corporate—position on marriage in an interview. Suddenly we saw city leaders threatening to punish Cathy's business by banning Chick-fil-A stores from Chicago and Boston.[14]

During the 2013 Christmas season, attacks were fired at Operation Christmas Child, an international evangelical ministry that sends shoe boxes filled with goodies and the story of Jesus to impoverished children. The American Humanist Association (AHA) sent letters to schools in Colorado and South Carolina threatening lawsuits unless they abandoned participation in the shoe box project.[15] Thankfully Colorado parents and local churches privately moved forward with the shoe box collections and even organized a "Religious Rights Rally" to expose the AHA's bully tactics.[16]

Hobby Lobby, Little Sisters of the Poor, and Liberty University are just a few of the faith-based institutions affected by the Affordable Care Act's employer mandate. Had the Supreme Court not ruled in Hobby Lobby's favor, the federal law would have forced faith-based institutions to either provide contraception, sterilization, and abortion-inducing drugs within their insurance coverage or pay a crippling penalty of $100 per employee, per day.[17]

Volumes upon volumes have been written about historical and present-day Christian persecution, making it impossible to cover every pertinent matter within the confines of one chapter. For this reason I will simply say this: Christian persecution abounds, and it is here in America. We evangelicals cannot take our cues from those who would have us give up our religious freedom to promote "love," "fairness," and "equality." If we do, we won't have to explain the difference between Christian persecution here and the tyranny believers face in other nations—because the climate will be much the same.

Do Christians Exaggerate Persecution?

Comedy Central's clever host Jon Stewart pretends attacks on Christians' religious freedoms do not exist. During a monologue on his *Daily Show,* Stewart mused, "Does anyone know…does the Christian persecution complex have an expiration date? Because…uh…you've all been in charge pretty much since…uh…what was that guy's name…Constantine? He converted in, what was it, 312 AD. I'm just saying, enjoy your success."[18]

Criticizing a so-called "persecution complex" is one of the Left's favorite ploys. Here the Left argues that Christians make false claims of martyrdom in order to hoist their identity and mission above others'.

Candida Moss, University of Notre Dame professor of New Testament and early Christianity, reignited the persecution complex debate with her new book, *The Myth of Persecution: How the Early Christians Invented a Story of Martyrdom.* According to Moss, "[Persecution] is a story that has brought comfort to the suffering, sick and oppressed, but it is a story that was used—expanded, exaggerated and even invented—to exclude heretics, that legitimized great violence and that continues to disrupt civil discourse."[19]

Christian persecution is no fairy tale. Despite the agenda-riddled scrutiny Moss and other secular academics promote, Christians cannot disregard the historical persecution of the early church recorded within the Word of God. Just turn to the Book of Acts for a breakdown of the torture suffered by the early church.

Before Stephen became the first Christian to die for his faith, he was an administrator in charge of the Jerusalem church's food-distribution program. He was also a teacher and a great speaker, and he performed miracles through the Holy Spirit. For this he was hated by men from the Synagogue of Freed Slaves (Acts 6:8–11). He cared for the poor, yes. But he wasn't afraid to boldly share his new faith in the public square.

Right before his stoning, Stephen spoke about the persistent persecution of believers, exclaiming, "You stubborn people! You are heathen at heart and deaf to the truth!...Name one prophet your ancestors didn't persecute! They even killed the ones who predicted the coming of the Righteous One—the Messiah whom you betrayed and murdered" (Acts 7:51-52, NLT).

Stephen was the first martyr, but he certainly wasn't the last Christian to be persecuted for his faith. Soon after Stephen's stoning, the apostle James, the brother of John, was killed at the direction of King Herod Agrippa. Later on, "When Herod saw how much this pleased the Jewish people, he also arrested Peter" (Acts 12:3, NLT). Thanks to divine intervention, Peter was eventually released from his prison cell (Acts 12:6–9).

We know that before his conversion, the apostle Paul was a traveling tormentor of Christians after a "wave of persecution" scattered the church of Jerusalem far and wide (Acts 8:2–3). But the traveling persecutor was transformed into a traveling preacher. Paul was stoned, whipped, imprisoned, and eventually martyred for his faith.

Claims such as Moss's do more than challenge assertions about persecution in the United States. They belittle the plight of tortured Christians around the world. Instead of making light of their suffering, popular culture and academia should be raising greater awareness. But why should they, when many Christians are also ignoring the threats, kidnappings, and killings many of their brothers and sisters in Christ face nearly every day.

The Face of the Persecuted Church

The Western world's quick and passionate response to Malala Yousafzai, the sixteen-year-old Pakistani Muslim girl who survived an attack on her life for advancing girls' education, is refreshing. Malala was invited to address the United Nations and join Jon Stewart on his *Daily Show*, and she received several phone calls and a visit from President Obama. But this brave young woman's story led me to raise a question, "If Malala was a Christian standing up for girls' right to believe in Jesus, would her attack have received the same international praise?" Sadly, we know that answer is no.

When you hear the term "the persecuted church," imagine the faces of three little Indonesian girls beheaded while walking to their Christian school in 2005.[20] Or the seven Egyptian Coptic Christians killed on a beach in Libya.[21] Or the Iraqi Christians attacked and harassed in Kurdistan (northern Iraq), a place where they once found asylum.[22]

According to the *New York Post*, in Syria an offshoot of al Qaeda has forced Christians in the northern city of Raqqa to pay for their protection. Under the agreement, "the Christians cannot renovate churches, display crosses, read Scripture too loudly, perform religious ceremonies outside of the church or sell pork or alcohol and must pay a twice-a-year special tax equivalent to hundreds of dollars per individual." Those who refuse the terms must either convert to Islam or "face the sword."[23]

Asia Bibi is a Pakistani Christian woman currently sitting on death row. After being dragged through the streets of her village, pelted with stones, and beaten by Muslim extremists, she was asked to either convert to Islam or face death.[24] Asia remains in prison because she refused to renounce her faith.

In Iran pastor and American citizen Saeed Abedini is being held in one of the country's most infamous prisons for practicing his Christian faith. His health is deteriorating, and US officials have shown little public concern. Observers have noted that while the White House issued numerous urgent calls for the release of two American hikers imprisoned in Iran in 2009, it has made few mentions of Pastor Saeed. Saeed's wife, Naghmeh, and the American Center for Law and Justice spend countless hours on public airwaves and in print seeking justice for Pastor Saeed, who was told by his captors that he might be released if he renounced his faith in Christ.[25]

On its face America still appears to be a glimmering beacon of religious freedom. But for the international persecuted church, things are growing much worse—and that is partly because the United Nations, the White House, and yes, even some Western Christians mistakenly signal a green light to abusers with our woeful silence.

The Left's Trojan Horse

Just as mainline churches have done for years, the evangelical Left downplays or manipulates the persecution of Christians to fit their own agenda. Rather than speaking out against Islamic or communist regimes that torture, imprison, or murder Christians, the religious Left tends to bring up international Christian persecution only when they want to belittle conservative Christians.

When conservative advocates voice their opposition to such

things as Christian bakery owners being forced to bake same-sex wedding cakes, the evangelical Left swoops in and tells us to hush and stop comparing our plight with that of persecuted Christians abroad. But when the dustup settles, the evangelical Left is otherwise silent about religious persecution or, worse, soft on regimes that terrorize believers, as Carl Medearis was at the 2013 Simply Jesus conference. (See chapter 3.) This does little to help persecuted believers.

Christian poet Armando Valladares became the recipient of IRD's 1983 Religious Freedom Award after serving twenty-two years for his faith in Fidel Castro's torturous Isla de Pinos Prison.[26] In his powerful acceptance speech, recorded in IRD's newsletter *Christianity and Democracy*, Valladares described the betrayal prisoners such as himself felt when they learned of mainline churches that downplayed their plight. He said:

> During those years, with the purpose of forcing us to abandon our religious beliefs and demoralize us, the Cuban communist indoctrinators repeatedly used the statements of support for Castro's revolution made by some represen-tatives of American Christian churches. Every time that a pamphlet was published in the United States, every time a clergyman would write an article in support of Fidel Castro's dictatorship, a translation would reach us and that was worse for the Christian political prisoners than the beatings or the hunger.[27]

Liberal evangelicals often exploit the international Christian persecution as a Trojan horse. Last year there was a wave of criti-cism leveled toward conservative evangelicals, who were accused of being more concerned with boycotting stores that did not say "Merry Christmas" than with addressing the horrors com-mitted against Christians throughout the world. In an article titled "In the Middle East, Not America, Christians Are Actually

Persecuted," popular, young faith-and-culture writer Jonathan Merritt made the claim that "American Christians have a persecution complex." If international persecution was truly his focal point, perhaps, "Sudanese Christians face genocide" would have been a better launching point. But Merritt's goal to deride Christians who see religious liberty infringements taking place here at home was made clear as he continued:

> Whenever a public figure criticizes the Christian movement or offers believers in other faiths an equal voice in society, you can bet Christians will start howling....But what is happening in America is not "persecution." Using such a label is an insult to the faithful languishing in other parts of the world where persecution actually exists—places like the Middle East.[28]

Merritt concludes his article by claiming the "true" war on religion is one "too few American Christians seem willing to enlist in."[29] Though I would be the last to say conservative evangelicals are getting this mission perfectly right, I work alongside individuals who have spent decades advocating for persecuted believers. I see their tireless efforts, and they are not alone, but Merritt is right, there should be far more in the fight. So where are those oh-so-concerned progressive evangelicals?

In a blog written around the same time as Merritt's, Brian McLaren admitted that he has not been very outspoken about international religious persecution. In his attempt to uncover why the world, and especially the Christian world, is so silent on this issue, McLaren also took jabs at conservatives with his six possible reasons for Christians' inaction. He claimed Christians are not speaking up about persecution because:

1. They don't want to add their voices to the growing
   numbers of Islamophobic voices in the Christian
   community....

2. They already know that much anti-Christian violence is retaliation against hawkish American for-
   eign policy....

3. Many Christians know that a careless bias against
   Palestinians—many of whom, by the way, are
   committed Christians—has become a pre-requisite
   in some circles for being considered "pro-Israel."...

4. American Christians are part of a global oil-based
   economy, and as such...depend on repressive
   Muslim governments...

5. Many...have accepted superficial clichés ("They
   are evil" or "Their religion is evil") and avoided
   the hard, often unsettling work of understanding
   how religious identity can be turned to violent
   ends—in any religion: Muslim, Christian, Jewish,
   Hindu, even atheist....

6. We don't know what can be done practically.[30]

A former graduate-school chum of McLaren's, Faith
McDonnell is IRD's long-serving director of religious liberty programs. After dedicating thirty years to working with grassroots
groups addressing Christian persecution and drafting legislation
related to religious persecution for the Episcopal Church and
the US Congress, McDonnell was disappointed with her friend
McLaren for echoing the "Religious Left's longstanding discom-
fiture on the issue of the persecuted Church and its tendency to
criticize persecuted Christians' defenders."[31] In her response to
McLaren's blog, McDonnell didn't mince words:

> You can't have it both ways. McLaren is concerned that
> too many Christians are silent about…"Christians in
> the Middle East and Africa…being slaughtered, tor-
> tured, raped, kidnapped, beheaded, and forced to flee the
> birthplace of Christianity" and yet he implies that those
> Christians who do speak up are "Islamaphobes."[32]

One week after the evangelical Left launched their "antigay"
and "discrimination" charges against fellow American Christians
who refuse to surrender religious liberty in order to appease our
critics, two young homosexual men were tortured and hanged in
Islamist Iran. The *Washington Free Beacon* was one of the only
news outlets to report on these two men who were sentenced to
death for "perversion" and crimes "insulting the prophet."[33]

As I write this chapter, it has only been two weeks since the
furor over the so-called gay discrimination amendments erupted.
It's saddening that none of the bloggers who so fervently criticized conservative evangelicals' concerns about religious liberty
infringements noted Iran's travesty. Not one of the influential
leaders I could find—not Brian McLaren, Tony Jones, or Rachel
Held Evans—hurled disapproving blog posts at Islam for its mur-
derous actions toward humanity.

The liberal evangelical blogosphere's silence speaks to their
efforts to herald their own progressive ideologies. To them, it
is better not to upset Islamic nations than to admit orthodox
Christians get something right when we speak up. But millions
of other believers will not keep quiet.

What's the Cost?

It is our duty as Christians to speak out about religious liberty
infringements here in the United States and the religious persecution taking place throughout the world. The blind spot for many
evangelicals is that in their desire to engage in less contentious

social problems, they rebuke the work of their brothers and sisters who are called to face the tough issues.

We cannot wait for the religious liberty battle to become less controversial. We will be waiting a long time.

Think about how much easier life would have been for Paul and Barnabas had they avoided Iconium, a city where some Jews "poisoned the minds of the Gentiles" against them (Acts 14:2, NLT). Still, Scripture tells us that Paul and Barnabas "stayed there a long time, preaching boldly about the grace of the Lord" (Acts 14:3, NLT).

If Paul and Barnabas had simply stayed in Jerusalem, preached quietly to other believing Jews, and peacefully fed the poor, today we "Gentiles" probably wouldn't personally know the Savior named Jesus. In addition, the apostles would have ignored God's calling on their lives—the same calling that every Christian has to publicly glorify God.

Had Paul and Barnabas avoided the tough cities, they probably would have never faced resentment, discrimination, and the harsh critics who sought their death. But their calling was not an easy one. It took courage and boldness. This is the face of Christianity. This is the reality of evangelizing. Though we may speak in love, the message we present will not always earn us love if we do it right.

Going to bat for the persecuted church takes extra courage. To defend persecuted Christians, you must speak out against despotic regimes and oppressive religions. To popular culture this is not politically correct, but that doesn't mean efforts such as these are not valuable and urgent.

Again, this is not to say that issues such as human trafficking are not important. Admittedly human trafficking has always been an advocacy issue close to my heart. But evangelicals cannot disregard religious freedom or life or the redefinition of marriage as less important than social justice issues that are not as contentious. Christ is the ultimate answer to every social ill.

Religious liberty is a justice issue that is going in the wrong direction. For many Christians the question remains: Can we really make a difference in such a complex situation at home and abroad? The answer to that question is yes…and no. One person is not enough. But one person plus God can redeem a culture and save lives.

Let me give you a practical example. At the turn of the nineteenth century, Great Britain was in serious moral decline. Christianity was reduced to mere symbolism. Devious landlords profited from shabby slums. Alcoholism flourished. Family units crumbled. Children and women worked sixteen-hour days in dangerous, filthy factories. On top of all that, some three million Africans were being held in bondage through Britain's international slave trade.[34]

Of the many issues he could have taken on, a born-again man named William Wilberforce felt a burden to join the abolitionist cause. Heartsick over the evils of slavery, Wilberforce set out to abolish Great Britain's destructive slave trade. He debated the need to end slavery in Parliament for years—to no avail.

In his efforts to end Britain's slave trade, Wilberforce suffered through hostile resistance. How could he avoid it? He was speaking out against a popular and lucrative establishment. But this did not stop him. In a gesture that brought great encouragement, Christian theologian John Wesley wrote to Wilberforce, telling him, "Unless God has raised you up for this very thing, you will be worn out by the opposition of men and devils. But if God be for you, who can be against you? Are all of them together stronger than God? O be not weary of well doing!"[35]

It isn't easy to speak God's truth when public opinion is against you. But as Wesley said, we cannot be weary in well-doing. Depending on God, Wilberforce continued to pressure Parliament to end slavery. It took twenty years, but in 1807 the Slave Trade Act finally put an end to the shipping and selling of human beings.

Following Christ without compromise comes at a cost. Sharing the gospel unabashedly, rejecting mediocre Christianity, and opposing the genocide of Christians around the world are not comfortable tasks. But Jesus told us that following Him wouldn't be easy.

Just as the world hated Christ, we can expect Christians to be despised. So it is vital that evangelicals continue on, boldly drawing strength from the words of our Lord, who said: "Blessed are you when people insult you, persecute you and falsely say all kinds of evil against you because of me. Rejoice and be glad, because great is your reward in heaven, for in the same way they persecuted prophets who were before you" (Matt. 5:11–12, NIV).

Chapter 9

SUPPORTING ISRAEL

> *Now, when I hear that Christians are*
> *getting together in order to defend the*
> *people of Israel, of course it brings joy*
> *to my heart. And it simply says, look,*
> *people have learned from history.*[1]
> — ELIE WIESEL

CROUCHED IN A SECRET HIDING PLACE, JEWISH REFUGEES found safe harbor during the Holocaust in the home of a Dutch Christian family named the ten Booms. Unfortunately, the Gestapo (Nazi secret police) persisted in its mission to exterminate every Jewish man, woman, and child, and in 1944 the courageous ten Boom family was found out.

Sisters Corrie and Betsie ten Boom were separated from their elderly father and eventually sent to Ravensbrück concentration camp. According to Corrie, while still in the concentration camp God told her and Betsie that, "It is for My people you must suffer this."[2]

Suffer the Christian women did. Clutching to their smuggled Bible, Corrie and Betsie endured lice, fleas, sickness, and beatings in the concentration camp. Tragically Betsie died of anemia in Ravensbrück. Corrie survived and spent the rest of her life preaching the gospel until her death in 1983.

Corrie and her family's legacy continue to inspire an evangelical woman named Susan Sandager. Susan travels the nation sharing the ten Booms' passion for God's chosen people and warning against Christian apathy toward Israel. Sandager explains:

> Miss ten Boom's message speaks volumes to the Church about how a true Christian should relate to Israel and God's People. Her family modeled Christ's example of laying down one's life for another. The ten Boom family shows us how to love Israel unconditionally. Like Ruth said to Naomi, the ten Booms said to the Jews, "Where you go, I go." The Church may miss her highest calling if she does not prepare herself to say also to Israel when and if the time ever comes, "Where you die, I will die."[3]

Cruelty and humiliation. Heat and cold. Silence and screaming. Disease and death. This generation cannot know firsthand what the Jewish people suffered in Nazi Germany and elsewhere during the Holocaust. In fact, our understanding of the history of the Jewish nation is thin. Most of us know only that a tiny Jewish nation-state exists today and that it has many, many enemies.

Unfortunately, I fear another dangerous trend is emerging within American evangelical circles. It is becoming unpopular to be a Christian Zionist and deemed uncompassionate to support Israel.

Because many of us Millennial evangelicals grew up in churches where support of Israel was expected without explanation, there are gaps in our understanding of the Jewish history, land rights, and theology that a Palestinian liberation movement has been able to seize upon. So before we can issue the clarion call to stand side by side with the only nation-state established by God, we must first answer three key questions: Why must Christians support Israel? Why is evangelical support for the Jewish nation declining? And, for that matter, when and why did Christians start supporting Israel in the first place?

Why Christians Must Support Israel

To avoid getting bogged down by all the fuzzy arguments presented by the evangelical Left and beyond, young and seasoned evangelicals need to have a firm, biblical grasp on why God has a soft spot for the Jewish people and a predetermined fate for the nation-state of Israel.

John Hagee, founder of Christians United for Israel (CUFI) and senior pastor of Cornerstone Church in San Antonio, Texas, identifies several key biblical reasons Christians are to stand in defense of the Jewish nation-state. Keep in mind:

1. Israel is the only nation created by a sovereign act of God.

2. Christians' support of Israel brings the blessing of God to them personally.

3. Christians owe a debt of eternal gratitude to the Jewish people for their contributions, including birthing the Christian faith.

4. God judges the Gentiles for their treatment of the Jews.[4]

As Pastor Hagee points out, Israel was birthed by God in a contract with Abraham. A contract is a promise, and God does not break His promises. Period. Don't take my word for it. Turn to Genesis chapter 12, and there you will see what is called the Abrahamic covenant between God and man.

In every contract both parties commit to carry out their part of the agreement. But typically one party must act first before the other can provide his promised goods. In the Abrahamic covenant or contract God told Abraham (then still referred to as Abram), "Leave your native country, your relatives, and your father's family and go to the land that I will show you" (Gen. 12:1, NLT). This was Abraham's part of the deal. He had to leave his comfort zone—everything he knew as home.

When Abraham followed through with God's instructions, God said: "I will make you into a great nation. I will bless you and make you famous, and you will be a blessing to others. I will bless those who bless you and curse those who treat you with contempt" (Gen. 12:2–3, NLT). The contract was laid out plain and simple.

God was not vague when He established the nation of Israel. Besides promising a Jewish nation, God set the parameters for the nation-state. Flip over to Genesis 15, and you'll see that God outlines certain boundaries: "I have given this land to your descendants, all the way from the border of Egypt to the great Euphrates River—the land now occupied by the Kenites, Kenizzites, Kadmonites, Hittites, Perizzites, Rephaites, Amorites, Canaanites, Girgashites, and Jebusites" (vv. 18–21, NLT).

So Abraham left his home and made the journey. It was a tough trip to say the least. Abraham's whole clan left what is modern-day southeast Iraq, traveled up into Syria, and then down into what we know as Israel. Scripture says Abraham and his family traveled to the land of Canaan, already inhabited by Canaanites and the other tribes listed above. Still, God told Abraham:

> I will confirm my covenant with you and your descendants after you, from generation to generation. This is the ever-lasting covenant: I will always be your God and the God of

> your descendants after you. And I will give the entire land
> of Canaan, where you now live as a foreigner, to you and
> your descendants. It will be their possession forever, and I
> will be their God.
> —GENESIS 17:7–8, NLT

This is where things got messy for Abraham's brood. He had two sons: Ishmael and Isaac. Ishmael would father the Arab (Palestinian) people, and Isaac would father the Israelites (the Jewish people). Are you wondering which descendants God's covenant belongs to? Well, the Lord told Abraham that his elderly wife, Sarah, would have a son. Sarah laughed in disbelief that she would ever have a child. Then after waiting years for their promised son, Sarah and Abraham took matters into their own hands. Abraham took the slave Hagar and conceived a son with her. That child was named Ishmael. (Note: Again, the fact that a human action is recorded in the Bible does not mean God endorses it. I wish more of my spiritual mentors had explained this to me when I was young.)

However, God told Abraham plainly that he and *Sarah* would have a child.

> Then Abraham bowed down to the ground, but he laughed
> to himself in disbelief. "How could I become a father at the
> age of 100?" he thought. "And how can Sarah have a baby
> when she is ninety years old?" So Abraham said to God,
> "May Ishmael live under your special blessing!"
> But God replied, "No—Sarah, your wife, will give birth
> to a son for you. You will name him Isaac, and I will con-
> firm my covenant with him and his descendants as an
> everlasting covenant. As for Ishmael, I will bless him also,
> just as you have asked. I will make him extremely fruitful
> and multiply his descendants. He will become the father of
> twelve princes, and I will make him a great nation. But my

covenant will be confirmed with Isaac, who will be born to
you and Sarah about this time next year."

—Genesis 17:17–21, NLT

God kept His promise, and Abraham and Sarah indeed had
a son they named Isaac. Genesis 21:12 tells us, "Isaac is the son
through whom your descendants will be counted" (NLT). The
land of Israel belongs to God, and He gave it to Abraham, Isaac,
and their descendants "as an everlasting possession" (Gen. 17:8,
NKJV). As Pastor Hagee bluntly states, "Ishmael, father of Arabs,
was excluded from the title deed to the land in Genesis 17:19–21.
Therefore, modern-day Palestinians have no biblical mandate to
own the land."[5]

As American Christians we have a part in the Abrahamic
covenant too. God said in Genesis 12:3 that He would treat
nations according to the way they treat Israel. Since World War
II and the re-creation of modern-day Israel, America has been
her loyal friend. President Bill Clinton once said: "America and
Israel share a special bond. Our relationship is unique among all
nations. Like America, Israel is a strong democracy, a symbol of
freedom, and an oasis of liberty, a home to the oppressed and
persecuted."[6] It is no coincidence that America saw incredible
prosperity after World War II and into the twenty-first century.
God always keeps His promises.

Pro-Palestine, Pro-Israel, Pro-Peace?

Israel's foes are smart. Islamic pro-Palestinian strategies have
swiftly swerved toward America's evangelicals. Here's the reason:
82 percent of white evangelicals believe God gave Israel to the
Jewish people, according to a 2013 study by the Pew Research
Center.[7] Unfortunately, the evangelical Left is rushing to help
swing the pendulum on this issue too.

According to the Committee for Accuracy in Middle East

Reporting in America (CAMERA), the Telos Group, a nonprofit supposedly dedicated to transforming the Israeli-Palestinian conflict, is one of the driving forces behind the new evangelical Palestinian liberation cause. The CAMERA report said, "Under the guise of being pro-everyone, pro-peace and pro-justice, this movement is moving Evangelicals away from their historic position of support for Israel toward unreflective support for the Palestinian cause."[8]

A prominent Telos Group adviser is Lynne Hybels, cofounder of the Chicago megachurch Willow Creek Community Church (where Shane Claiborne served an internship). Hybels is an outspoken pro-Palestine activist who also uses the "pro-everyone" rhetoric. She wrote, "When I say I'm pro-Israeli, I mean that I support the existence of the State of Israel as a home for the Jewish people.... When I say I'm pro-Palestinian, I mean that I believe the Palestinians have an equally valid right to live in the land and should have the same civil rights that are afforded to Israeli Jewish citizens, whether that's in one state, two states, or however many states."[9] And while she hopes that one day Jews and Arabs will live "peacefully and equally as brother and sisters," she thinks Israel's "ongoing military occupation of the West Bank and the continuing blockade of Gaza is a violation of human rights."[10]

Hybels's "pro-everyone" ambitions may be well-intentioned, but IRD President Mark Tooley raises an important question: "How do evangelicals like Hybels suggest reaching peace with a people who largely do not want to co-exist with their adversaries?" Tooley countered, "They never say. Instead, they focus on the injustice of Israel's occupation, while granting that Palestinian violence is also bad."[11]

Hybels's and others' pro-Palestinian cause is commendable but disingenuous. All too often the pro-Palestinian monologue paints Israel as an oppressive, violent bully and Palestinians as

innocent, meek underdogs. The Christ at the Checkpoint conference (CATC) that takes place in Bethlehem every other year is a
perfect example of what is happening among the growing anti-
Israel Christian crowd. CATC chooses to focus on political and
social critiques of Israel rather than on what God's Word has
sketched out for the nation.

IRD reporter Luke Moon attended both the 2012 and 2014
CATC conferences. Luke told me, "Over the last four years the
leaders and participants of Christ at the Checkpoint have become
increasingly astute to the nature of American evangelicals and
how best to reach them with their narrative of Palestinian
oppression at the hands of Israel."[12]

In previous years evangelical Left leaders such as Lynne
Hybels, Shane Claiborne, and Tony Campolo have been key
CATC speakers. Interestingly, the 2014 conference was different.
Popular evangelical Left authors and speakers were noticeably
absent. Presumably, organizers recognized that to win over the
mainstream evangelical community, you cannot go through the
evangelical Left. Internally, evangelical Left leaders have a hard
time agreeing on their own beliefs and values stemming from
the fact that their distorted theologies possess too many holes.
So in 2014 CATC cleverly turned their focus to evangelical university professors and students.

Instead of Lynne Hybels, Wheaton College professor Gary
Burge, PhD, was a notable session speaker. However, his perspective did not vary much from Hybels's. In his address Dr.
Burge encouraged "replacement theology," which argues that
God's promises to the Jewish people were fulfilled in Christ
and He is no longer concerned about certain nations occupying
specific parcels of land. Dr. Burge claimed, "[The apostle Paul]
leads me to think the promise of Abraham has been fulfilled in
Christ, and therefore those who attach themselves to Christ are

Abraham's children.... The Holy Land then is the entire globe and is no longer the privilege of an ethnic few."[13]

Students, especially from Wheaton and Azusa Christian Pacific University, attended the conference as part of what are unofficially dubbed "protest tours." Columnist David Greenfield wittily noted that protest tours are what American leftist college students take to feel more humanitarian toward Palestinians.[14] The tours show students only one narrow perspective of the Israel-Palestinian conflict—the peaceful Palestinian side. Students visit impoverished Palestinian families, peaceful Muslim Arabs, and the token Palestinian orphanage. The one-sided view, however, lends to an increased resentment toward Jewish Israelis.

While in Bethlehem Luke Moon spoke with Jason, a student participating in Dr. Burge's tour. Jason told Luke that he grew up in an evangelical church and always heard the Israeli narrative but wanted to see the Palestinian liberation view for himself. Seeming to take joy in undermining Christian Zionism, Jason told Luke all about the oppressed Palestinians he met along his journey.

Amused, Luke asked Jason how many Israeli families he had met on his tour. "Two," Jason answered. One was a Jewish Israeli who had spent five months in jail for refusing to serve in Israel's military. The other was Jason's bus driver. "Hardly the well-rounded education tour worthy of being connected with such a prestigious Christian school [as Wheaton]," Luke observed.[15]

After attending CATC and extensive consultations with both Israelis and Palestinians, Luke concluded, "Palestinians know that evangelicals are the last bastion of support within the West. If they can get evangelicals to cave, then Israel is done."[16]

United Against Israel

Hollywood film director Steven Spielberg once said, "As a Jew I am aware of how important the existence of Israel is for the survival of us all. And because I am proud of being Jewish, I am worried by the growing anti-Semitism and anti-Zionism in the world."[17] Some Christians will bury their heads in the sand on this controversial topic, but even the secular world can see the unified efforts against the Jewish state of Israel are getting stronger.

To squash any potential for anti-Semitic accusations, the evangelical Left touts a two-state solution because it sounds *diverse* and *peaceful*. Sometimes this proposed solution is called divestment. Basically, divestment calls for Israel to surrender the West Bank and Gaza Strip. What's wrong with their rather vague solution is that few inside Israel or Palestine are truly considering this resolution. Only the West is talking about divestment. Arab Palestinians and Jewish Israelis each have a clear, unwavering objective: the right of return or a Jewish nation-state.

Lacking adequate geopolitical understanding of this issue, evangelicals continue their pro-Palestine stance. As they grow and strengthen, these sentiments help foster a global bias against the Jews.

The major problem liberal evangelicals refuse to recognize is that their good-hearted Palestinian liberation cause leads to anti-Jewish discrimination. While it is highly doubtful that Hybels and other prominent pro-Palestine leaders are prejudiced against the Jewish people, they are walking young evangelicals perilously close to the line of anti-Semitism. The real danger is growing as the evangelical Left watches young evangelicals grow critical and even resentful of the Jewish people, and influential leaders say nothing.

Anti-Jewish discrimination is under way, and it is more brutal than the evangelical Left cares to admit. Before Palestinian Liberation Organization (PLO) leader Yasser Arafat died in 2004, he explained, "We plan to eliminate the State of Israel and establish a purely Palestinian state. We will make life unbearable for Jews by psychological warfare and population explosion."[18]

Lest we be blindsided by the well-intentioned and compassionate-sounding arguments for Palestinians, know that Jews have faced unimaginable oppression and cruelty at the hands of their Arab neighbors. Refugees of Arab oppression, the Jews were forced to return home. I'm not just talking about European refugees after the Holocaust. Oh, no, there was much discrimination within the Middle East. After World War II, Muslim or Arab countries surrounding the land of Israel expelled hundreds of thousands of Jews from their homes. Sadly, few on the Left ever talk about these oppressors.[19]

Thankfully, Lela Gilbert, author of *Saturday People, Sunday People*, did a remarkable job outlining this anti-Semitic discrimination. Sometimes called the "Forgotten Exodus," nearly a million Jewish refugees were pushed out of their homes between 1920 and 1970 and settled in Israel. Gilbert lays out the stark numbers:

- Iraq: In 1948 there were one hundred thirty-five thousand Jews. Less than ten are left today.

- Yemen and Aden: In 1948 there were sixty-three thousand Jews. Today there are less than two hundred fifty.

- Syria and Lebanon: In 1948 there were thirty thousand Jews. Twenty-five Jews are left in Syria and likely fewer in Lebanon.

- Egypt: In 1948 there were one hundred thousand Jews. Today there are less than one hundred.

- Libya: In 1948 there were thirty-eight thousand Jews. Today no Jews are believed to live in Libya.[20]

After they were pushed out of their homeland and then expelled from neighboring counties, the first female Israeli prime minister, Golda Meir, explained the Jewish nation's plight well when she said, "We Jews have a secret weapon in our struggle with the Arabs; we have no place to go."[21]

Living in an era when information about Israel's history and the Jewish people's plight can be accessed with the touch of our fingertips, it is shocking that both are belittled on American soil. Support for Israel is a "dirty word" on many American college campuses. Anti-Semitism on California's public university campuses was so widespread among faculty and students that in 2011 the state had to create a task force called the California Assembly Select Committee on Campus Climate to investigate. The committee held a hearing, and several Jewish students offered gripping testimonies.[22]

University of California at Los Angeles (UCLA) student Omer Hit testified: "We were told that by opposing divestment, we are tying Jewish identity to oppression, racism, and human rights violations—an extremely dehumanizing accusation which silences and caricatures our actual concerns about the issue.... We constantly hear the term 'Zionist' use as a dirty word... And worst of all, we heard speakers attempt to put down our objections by falsely redefining the term 'anti-Semitism,' extending it beyond hatred of Jews."[23] Hit went on to say that attempting to change the meaning of anti-Semitism "effectively minimizes the 1,900 year history of racism and oppression targeted specifically against Jews in Europe, the Middle East, and elsewhere."[24]

UC Berkeley student Avi Levine made this observation: "Just because someone is allowed to say something doesn't mean that we need to tacitly endorse it. That's what we need from our leadership. We need to be able to, when there is a hateful divestment resolution that's labeling me as a Zionist Nazi when my grandfather has a number tattooed to his arm, to say that this is not OK.... It's not acceptable and we don't stand by it. That's what we need from our leadership."[25]

Beware the United Nations too. The international forum (desperate for power) is seething with disdain for Israel. Since its conception in 2006, the UN Human Rights Council has demonstrated anti-Semitic bias by consistently passing anti-Israel resolutions while overlooking certain violations by Iran, Pakistan, and Syria. According to UN Watch, an organization dedicated to promoting human rights by monitoring the international forum, the UN Human Rights Council "criticized Israel on 27 separate occasions, in resolutions that grant effective impunity to Hamas, Hezbollah and their state sponsors."[26]

You know it's bad too when even the UN's former secretary-general Kofi Annan notices the Human Rights Council's "disproportionate focus on violations by Israel."[27]

UN Watch also noted that, "Obsessed with condemning Israel, the Council in its first year failed to condemn human rights violations occurring in any of the world's 191 other countries. In its second year, the Council finally criticized one other country when it 'deplored' the situation in Burma, but only after it censored out initial language containing the word 'condemn.' It even praised Sudan for its 'cooperation.'"[28]

The Palestinian Christians

Some evangelicals struggle with supporting the Jewish people in Israel when it seems to be at the expense of fellow Christians in Palestine. This is largely due to a slanted narrative created by the mainstream media and now the Christian Left that paints Palestinian Christians as victims and Israeli Jews as their oppressors. Palestinian Christians are certainly victimized but not by whom you might think.

According to the Institute for Middle East Understanding, 93 percent of Palestinians are Muslim and 6 percent are Christians.[29] Because of the large disparity between Muslims and Christians, Palestinian Christians are treated as second-class citizens by their own people.

Speaking to students at Sweden's Uppsala University, Christy Anastas, a young Palestinian Christian woman and trained lawyer, told of how she endured harassment, intimidation, and sexual abuse while growing up in Palestinian-controlled Bethlehem. "Israel doesn't kill us or threaten us for sharing our views," she said. "Palestinians do."[30]

Palestinian Christians are certainly affected by Israel's efforts to protect itself from terrorism, but they are not targeted. Christy noted this when she told of her childhood friend who was killed when Israelis confused her family's car with that of wanted Palestinian terrorists. Talking about her childhood friend's death, Christy said, "She was a Christian. This story has been told by the church and by my people to the whole world."[31]

A story gone largely untold is that of Christy's Christian uncle, who was killed for standing up against Palestinian Islamists. In Bethlehem Jews and Christians were pressured to pay protection money to Palestinian Islamists to secure safety during the fighting. "My uncle was one of these Christians in Bethlehem community who had to pay this money," Christy explained. "But sadly after a while him and other Christians started seeing these people who called themselves 'Freedom Fighters'—I call them mafia—they used to stand next to Christian houses, shoot and launch rockets at Israel, and run so that the response would come mainly on Christian houses."[32]

After Christy's uncle decided to stop paying the fee for supposed protection, Islamists accused him of being a traitor before shooting and killing him in front of his home. Another Christian man stood and spoke out against the Palestinian Islamists at her uncle's funeral. He was later shot in the head by Palestinian

Islamists. He lived, but he was left blind. "None of these stories and more were told by my people to the world," Christy said.

"So many people will tell you that the major factor is the Israeli occupation," she continued. "Well, I believe in facts and statistics." Christy went on to explain that during Bethlehem's Israeli occupation, the number of Palestinian Christians increased from 81 percent to 85 percent. The number of Christians in Bethlehem then decreased to 7 percent, according to Christy, after the two Intifadas, the uprising of the Palestinian Liberation Organization (PLO) and the terrorist group Hamas. "If the reason and the major factor is the Israeli occupation, why is it affecting the number of Christianity only?" asked the brave young woman.[33]

Christy also described how Palestinian Islamists are stealing Christian land and told of how women have utterly no rights in the eyes of the Palestinian authority. "I used to get sexually harassed going to university. I used to get to university and then turn around feeling disgusted, like almost walking in a zoo between animals," she said. "Sometimes I'd get home sitting in a minibus having people touching me. These are the rights that we have as women there."[34] Since sharing her story, Christy has been denounced by family members likely under pressure from Islamists, and she received death threats in the United Kingdom, where she now has political asylum.

By supporting Israel, understand that evangelicals are neither ignoring nor rejecting our fellow Palestinian sisters and brothers in Christ. Instead, we are supporting human dignity, freedom of religion, freedom of speech, women's rights, and democracy for all.

How to Support Israel Well

During graduate school I served a short stint with a pro-life non-governmental organization present at the United Nations in New York City. While advocating for pro-life initiatives in various meetings, I was warned by my superiors to avoid the Israeli delegates. They were ardently pro-abortion and would have us pro-life advocates kicked out. In fact, our closest allies at the UN on the pro-life issue were Muslim state delegates. Iran loved us. It was quite a spooky twist.

At first the Israeli delegates' brashness left me frustrated and feeling almost betrayed by a nation I loved and supported. I thought, "How dare they try to kick us Christians out of a meeting? Don't they know we are on *their* side? Why support their efforts if they won't support mine?" I'll admit that my thought process was all wrong.

Still, many evangelicals approach support of Jews and Israel with an "I'll do what you want if you do what I want" attitude. Others view Israel as valuable only as a mission field. It is worth their time so long as Jews convert to Christianity. Neither approach is acceptable.

This was also the attitude of Muhammad, the creator of Islam. Muhammad's strategy was to present Islam as a peaceful religion in order to attract converts, especially the Jews. When his plan failed, he declared jihad, or holy war, on all infidels.[35] Obviously this is an extreme example, but it does clearly demonstrate a pitfall evangelicals need to avoid. If we are going to support Israel, then we must support the Jewish nation-state well. A half-hearted, self-centered agenda will only do more harm than good.

This is not to say we evangelicals must not share the good news of Jesus the Messiah. I am saying only that our support of the Jewish nation-state should not be contingent upon conversion. Some Jewish Israelis have been hurt by placing their trust in evangelicals, who upon realizing conversion was a no-go abandoned their commitments to Israel and the Jews.

Robert Nicholson is a former fellow at the Tikvah Center in New York City and an author on Christian-Jewish relations. In a recent *Times of Israel* article titled "Who's Afraid of Christian

Zionism?" Nicholson pointed out the fears Jewish people have of evangelical support of Israel by highlighting his Israeli readers' comments. One person wrote:

> As a Jew/Israeli, I like the political support for Israel. But I do find the undercurrent drive to convert us, in that political support, disgusting. Martin Luther at first liked us. But when we didn't convert, he called on his followers to burn us.... Will they love us when we don't convert?[36]

Ouch. The comments reflecting distrust of evangelicals didn't stop there. Another comment read:

> I dislike the idea I must agree with evangelicals, whose main purpose is to convert me, because they support Israel.... Sorry, but why would I support or form a strategic alliance with someone who supports me only so far as it fits his purposes and, more than likely, would throw me under a bus if I didn't?[37]

Nicholson took the opportunity to explain, "As an evangelical who affirms both the 'Great Commission' *and* the right of the Jewish people to govern themselves in their ancient homeland (yes, it is possible to hold these two things in one's head at the same time), I would submit to my Jewish friends that they needn't fear."[38] Nicholson went on to list five helpful reasons Jewish people need not fear their evangelical neighbors:

1. Christian Zionism is not dependent on evangelizing.

2. Evangelicals believe that no one can become a Christian unless he or she demonstrates genuine, uncoerced faith in Jesus Christ.

3. The world is a marketplace of ideas where every human is able to accept whatever worldview he or she chooses.

4. Jews are capable of rejecting teachings when exposed to Christians.

5. For most Jews committed to Judaism, conversations with Christians strengthen their faith.[39]

Each of these may be inverted as healthy boundaries for well-intentioned evangelicals to keep in mind also. We cannot force people to believe in Christ, whether by private or public means. And as Nicholson goes on to explain, evangelicals must commit not only to a pro-Israel stance but also to a respectful attitude toward Jewish people everywhere. He notes, "Claiming to be pro-Israel abroad without showing ourselves to be pro-Jewish at home is more than just unfeeling; it's downright contradictory."[40] Christian Zionists should witness among the Jewish people, but conversion should not be the main reason we commit ourselves to Israel.

Consider once more the example of Corrie ten Boom and her family. The ten Booms risked their own lives to protect Jewish people. However, the ten Booms did not muzzle the gospel. They shared about Jesus the Messiah with the Jews in their home and in the concentration camps. But their love of the Jewish people did not end when their Jewish neighbors did not convert. American evangelicals must do the same.

Israel may be the Jewish people's birthright, but defending it is the Christian people's responsibility. To believe or act otherwise is to neglect our vulnerable Jewish neighbors and ignore God's Word.

PART THREE: PREVENTING THE COLLAPSE

> *Teach me your ways, O LORD,*
> *that I may live according to*
> *your truth! Grant me purity of*
> *heart, so that I may honor you.*
>
> PSALM 86:11, NLT

Chapter 10

SPEAKING TRUTH IN LOVE

> *I believe that unarmed truth and*
> *unconditional love will have the*
> *final word in reality. This is why*
> *right temporarily defeated is*
> *stronger than evil triumphant.*[1]
> — MARTIN LUTHER KING JR.

CHRISTIAN APOLOGIST RAVI ZACHARIAS PUT THE SITUATION plainly, "Our culture is flirting with all kinds of things.... People are struggling with the lines that are being blurred and erased. And you can be sure what G. K. Chesterton said is right, 'Whenever you remove any fence, always pause long enough to ask why it was put there in the first place.'"[2]

Stop and think about all the fences being torn down in our culture: fences around marriage, around the sanctity of life, around the inerrancy of Scripture, and around the very existence of God. Meanwhile the culture is building fences around churches that promote traditional Christian teachings and decrying them as intolerant. Honestly this is infuriating, and at times I just want to fire back with a snarky blog post or a harsh tweet. I struggle with this—I really do.

But, unfortunately, to angrily retaliate against those who mock and marginalize Christian beliefs is to kick the door closed on public discussion of faith. So what are evangelicals—young and old—to do in the face of ridicule and rejection? Wise mentors usually answer: "Speak truth with love and compassion." But how do we do that exactly?

I wrestled long and hard with this phrase, "speak the truth in love." It was introduced in the apostle Paul's instructions to the Ephesians, "Rather, speaking the truth in love, we are to grow up in every way into him who is the head, into Christ" (Eph. 4:15). In context Paul is writing to encourage unity and maturity within the body of believers. As they grow in their knowledge of Christ, Paul says, they will not be swayed by "every wind of new teaching" or "lies so clever they sound like the truth" (v. 14, NLT). Rather, they will "speak the truth in love, growing in every way more and more like Christ" (v. 15, NLT).

As I considered Paul's words, I couldn't help but wonder, "Which is more important, truth or love? Which is more like Christ?" The questions started to make my head spin, so I determined to meditate on this subject and ask the Almighty to show me what speaking the truth in love really looks like. Thanks to a series of divinely appointed talks, events, and new friends, I have been able to parse out an understanding that is much easier said than done.

Does Love Always Win?

These days many people mistake compassion for acceptance of things we know are morally wrong. To be compassionate toward those who are same-sex attracted, we should accept homosexuality. To be compassionate toward those facing an unintended pregnancy, we should allow abortion. To be compassionate toward those who practice other faiths, we should believe that all religious paths lead to God. "Speaking truth in love" is too often used to condone our silence on uncomfortable cultural issues, but this tact reflects a dangerous misunderstanding of the phrase—and it is self-centered. I'll explain.

In Jesus's longest-recorded teaching, the Sermon on the Mount, He told us that His followers must be the salt of the earth and the light of the world. Jesus said, "A city set on a hill cannot be hidden. Nor do people light a lamp and put it under a basket" (Matt. 5:14–15). In other words, if we aren't going to publicly share the gospel, what's the point? If Christians determine to hide what Jesus taught to avoid hurt feelings, then the world might not ever know His restorative love.

If you haven't already noticed, I love examples and learn best from illustrations. So, to demonstrate the idea of "salt and light" to my Sunday school class I broke off a lump of blue Play-Doh and handed it to each student. "Make something unique," I told them. "Be sure you each make something different."

As they created lovely hearts, crosses, peace signs, and snowmen, I rolled the remaining Play-Doh into a ball. Placing the dough ball in the center of the table, I said, "This is the world. Blue and boring, everything in it is the same. But your sculptures reflect your uniqueness as diverse followers of Christ."

Next, I went around the table and asked each student to tell me things that make it scary to share the gospel at school, on their sports teams, or with friends. Their answers included:

- "I'm afraid of fighting."

- "My friends might not want to be my friends anymore."

- "It might hurt other people's feelings."

After each hesitant answer, I asked the student to break off a piece of his sculpture and hand it over to me. As we continued to talk about reasons we compromise our principles, I meshed their broken pieces back into my dough ball. By the time they finished sharing their answers, you could no longer distinguish their unique sculptures from the rest of the world.

It is difficult to be different. It is frightening to talk about Jesus as the only way to salvation in a classroom mingled with Muslims and Hindus. Still, we can't keep our light hidden for fear of offending others. We can't decide to never mention hell because it sounds harsh. According to Proverbs 27:6, "Faithful are the wounds of a friend, but deceitful are the kisses of an enemy" (NAS). To love our friends and neighbors is to be honest about the hard stuff.

Consider finding out that your best friend suffers from a curable disease. Your friend has no idea a remedy exists, so he stops searching. You, on the other hand, learn about an easy-to-access cure that is totally free of cost. Would you hide the cure you found from your friend so as not to upset him? No! You love your friend. You are concerned about his fate, so you would call him or send a text message in all caps to shout out how he can get the cure. This is an example of speaking truth in love. You're giving your friend information he needs because you love him.

Why would sharing the good news of the gospel be any different? In fact, wouldn't the urgency to help a loved one find spiritual wholeness be even greater?

"There is an unloving way to speak truth," says Baptist pastor John Piper. "That kind of truth-speaking we should repudiate. But there is a way to speak the truth in love, and that we should seek. It is not always a soft way to speak, or Jesus would have to be accused of lack of love in dealing with some folks in the Gospels."[3]

Jesus's harsh words to the Pharisees, His straightforward

acknowledgment that the woman at the well was living in sin, and His loving restoration of the woman caught in adultery were all examples of Jesus speaking truth in love. Simply softening our tone is not evidence of love. Love breaks our hearts for those around us, and out of that heartbreak we are compelled to share the truth.

I cannot emphasize enough how important it is to possess love for those to whom you're directing truth. The verbal attacks can be harsh. But even in the heat of the "culture battles," we must respond in love. If the motivation for speaking truth is to make another feel foolish, then something has gone terribly wrong.

I think Christian mothers of unruly teenage daughters have a leg up on everyone else in the "speaking truth in love" department. I'm sure there are other real-world examples we could draw from, but when it comes to finding someone who knows how to reflect Christ's love in the heat of battle, I can think of no better model than my own mom. So with permission, I use her to illustrate this concept. By now you know the lies the world fed me and that I bought into in high school and college. But stubborn doesn't even come close to portraying my attitude against tradition, God, and my parents. Resentful is probably a better word.

Remembering how callous I was toward my mom is hard. But thank God she never once stopped sharing the truth, even when I argued that what she believed was not "truth" but merely her "interpretation" of Scripture. No, she never stopped reminding me of the authority of the Word of God—because she loved me. There were times when I resented her for it, but in the end, when I felt confused and hopeless, her voice reminded me of God's promises.

When I asked my mom how she balanced love and truth during those dark days, she responded: "Parents discipline because we love and show firmness for fear of the danger that comes when our kids make the wrong decisions. But if there was no authentic love, [but just] a yelling match, you wouldn't have received the truth. Without love, walls go up and defense mechanisms come out."

The nature of love is outlined in 1 Corinthians 13: "Love is patient and kind; love does not envy or boast; it is not arrogant or rude. It does not insist on its own way; it is not irritable or resentful; it does not rejoice at wrongdoing, but rejoices with the truth.... So now faith, hope, and love abide, these three; but the greatest of these is love" (vv. 4–6, 13).

The description of love in 1 Corinthians is a difficult standard to meet. No, I don't love without irritation or rudeness. (I'm working on it!) I may never love as perfectly as 1 Corinthians instructs. But I never stop praying that God would teach me to love others the way He does.

Christians must love others the way a parent loves a child. We must be genuinely burdened for the sin with which our neighbors are struggling. This kind of love comes from a devotion to Christ, not the world. As Hillsong United's song "Hosanna" says, let our hearts break with the things that break God's heart. May that be our prayer, because God the Father's heart breaks for all of His children, no matter their theology, political sway, or social status. If His heart breaks for the lost, so too should ours ache so much that we are motivated to stand up and speak out.

In the back alleys of New York City during the 1950s, drug lords and gang members were notorious for their guerrilla attacks. The tipping point came in July 1957, when teenage gang members ambushed and murdered a fifteen-year-old boy in a park.[4] The murder made headlines across the nation, highlighting not only the trial but also New York's growing gang problem.

A young Pennsylvania pastor named David Wilkerson happened to see an article about the young gang members' murder trial in *Life* magazine. "I started to flip the page over," Wilkerson said. "But as I did, something caught my eye. It was the eyes of a figure in the drawing—a boy. He was one of seven boys on trial for murder. I held the magazine closer to get a better look. The artist had captured a look of bewilderment, hatred and despair in the young boy's features. Suddenly, I began to cry."[5]

A love for New York's toughest gangs washed over Wilkerson. "I was dumbfounded by the next thought that sprang into my head," he said. "It came to me full-blown, as if from somewhere else: Go to New York and help those boys."[6]

With nowhere to stay and no contacts, Wilkerson drove into the city and slept in his car. But sharing the message of Jesus with drug addicts, prostitutes, and violent gang members proved more challenging than Wilkerson probably expected.

In the film adaptation of Wilkerson's autobiography, *The Cross and the Switchblade*, there is a scene I love. Wilkerson's character is trying to explain God's love to a hostile gang, and at one point the gang leader tells him, "You come near me, and I'll kill you!" Undaunted, Wilkerson's character replies, "Yeah, you could do that. You could cut me up into a thousand pieces and lay them in the street and every piece will still love you."[7]

Wilkerson's heart overflowed with compassion for these teens, and his message was a constant reminder to the city's "untouchables" that God loved them. Yet this in and of itself couldn't save them. Repentance of sins—leaving behind old ways and addictions through God's grace—is necessary for transformation. Because of his love Wilkerson condemned the gang's hate, drug abuse, stealing, and killing. Love is what pierced his heart with compassion for the gang—and it is what drove him to challenge them with the truth.

Because of Wilkerson's boldness, a notorious gang leader named Nicky Cruz found salvation in Jesus Christ. Cruz became an evangelist, and in time he founded Nicky Cruz Outreach, an evangelistic Christian ministry. What an inspiring example of how great change happens when we take our Christian witness beyond the church pews.

Even if you haven't heard the story of a country pastor named David Wilkerson, you probably have heard of Teen Challenge. Out of Wilkerson's bold commitment to preach the Word of God and his concern for his neighbors, one of the largest and most successful addiction-recovery programs in the nation was born.

As Wilkerson demonstrated, to speak "truth in love" the two cannot be separated. You cannot love your neighbors without telling them the truth about the consequences of their actions.

Does Truth Always Hurt?

It is a relief to learn that other evangelicals have struggled to figure out how to live out "truth in love." The Gospel Coalitions' Tony Reinke wrestled with this concept too, and he recounted his *"aha!"* moment in a blog post. Referring to Ephesians 4:15, he wrote: "I assumed that the verse meant only that when hard news or rebuke needed to be brought, it should be done with tenderness and sensitivity. I was wrong....At its core, we speak the truth in love when we care enough to speak the gospel into the lives of those around us."[8]

It might sound strange, but the biggest lesson I've learned in my study of this phrase is that to stifle truth in the name of love is actually quite selfish. Bruce Frohnen, a law professor at Ohio Northern University, observed that, "'Niceness' is a rather shallow set of habits and attitudes more concerned with comfort than engagement, ease than excellence, contentment than striving to do one's best....Unfortunately, when truth comes to be seen as subjective, toleration becomes the chief virtue, and it comes to mean simply ignoring one's fellows, in essence not caring what others do."[9] To hide from truth to be perceived as "nice" does no one any favors.

The truth does hurt, because it leads us to give up our crutches and depend on God. Just forty-eight days after Jesus's death and resurrection, Peter gave the first Christian sermon in Jerusalem. He surely didn't bow to "niceness." The Bible says that when the Jews heard Peter's message at Pentecost, they were "cut to the heart" (Acts 2:37). After hearing Peter's firm words, the Jews didn't get mad and stomp away as we might like to presume. Instead, they asked, "What shall we do?" Motivated by love, Peter told his neighbors, "Repent and be baptized every one of you in the name of Jesus Christ for the forgiveness of your sins" (v. 38).

Political correctness and "niceness" do not spread the gospel nor start great awakenings. Southern Baptist evangelist Billy Graham can attest. In March 1950, when his evangelistic crusades were at their height, Graham took his "repent and turn to God" message to South Carolina. We wonder today why forty thousand people packed into a local stadium just to hear Graham preach. Then we wonder again why two thousand people in one place on one Sunday came to salvation after hearing the simple message of the cross.[10]

Graham has reasoned, "The cross is offensive because it confronts people. Even so, it is a confrontation that all of us must face."[11] Being confronted with truth brings people to a crossroads. It challenges them to know Christ in a deeper way and receive an unconditional love the world will never be able to offer—no matter how hard it tries to convince us otherwise.

I've heard it said that Billy Graham's crusades drew such large crowds and led to so many salvations because the culture was less hostile to Christianity. I don't fully agree with this assessment. One reason I don't agree, believe it or not, is because of a story told by the religious Left's Rob Bell.

Before Bell transformed into a provocative spiritual writer and speaker, he was an evangelical pastor doing spectacular things for God's kingdom. During a conversation with the Very Reverend Jane Shaw of Grace Cathedral in San Francisco, Bell described how shocked he was by the church's response to his sermons on the "rules" laid out in the Old Testament.

Bell said: "For the first year and a half I preached the Book of Leviticus verse by verse by verse—and even more people came.... I'm like twenty-eight, twenty-nine...a thousand people, two thousand people, three thousand people, four thousand people, five thousand people, six thousand people, seven thousand people, eight thousand people." He continued, "I'm talking, like, a baptism service where we baptize some people, and people begin coming out of their chairs fully dressed, coming to the front and saying, 'Please baptize me! Whatever I am experiencing now, I have to be a part of this.' So you're baptizing a hundred, a hundred ten, a hundred twenty, a hundred thirty people at a time."[12]

In another eye-opening interview, this time with the *New Yorker*, Bell described his journey from founding Mars Hill Bible Church, which became a widely influential Michigan megachurch, to a dark place of doubting the inerrancy of Scripture and traditional evangelical views of God, Jesus, heaven, and hell. It was during that period that he began focusing his sermons on oppression, distorted social justice, and climate change. Church membership fell by the thousands.[13]

Jonathan Edwards's "Sinners in the Hands of an Angry God" is arguably one of America's most famous sermons. The message was delivered on July 8, 1741, in Enfield, Connecticut, in the midst of the Great Awakening. It is reported that Edwards did not speak with a severe, booming voice, nor did he employ theatrics, as we might imagine from the title. "He scarcely gestured or even moved," one observer wrote, "and he made no attempt by the elegance of his style or the beauty of his pictures to gratify the taste and fascinate the imagination."[14]

So why is Edwards's sermon one of the most remembered in our history despite the fact that he proclaimed, "The Wrath of

God burns against [sinners], their Damnation don't slumber, the Pit is prepared" and "The *Devil* stands ready to fall upon them and seize them as his own, at what Moment God shall permit him"?[15] Perhaps it is because he simply shared the truth. As cliché as it might sound, we know, in fact, that the truth sets us free (John 8:32).

Truth and Love Birth Revival

There are many more illustrations, but what better example of speaking truth in love is there to follow than Jesus? Go back to John 5:1–15 and reread the story of Jesus healing the lame man by the pool of Bethesda. It is it very important that you don't stop reading after the man's healing, because what happened next exemplifies a vital part of the character and mission of Jesus.

The man starts walking away from the pool when the Pharisees take notice and ask who healed him. The man didn't even know Jesus's name, and he didn't see Him because there was a crowd. Later Jesus sought the man out in the temple. Mind you, the man had been lame for thirty-eight years, so being able to walk was pretty momentous. But after Jesus healed the man, He went looking for him to say, "Now you are well; so stop sinning, or something even worse may happen to you" (John 5:13, NLT).

Jesus didn't warn that something "worse" may happen to condemn the man. It came from a place of genuine concern for the man's spiritual well-being. That is why Jesus—and those who follow in His footsteps—are to, in a spirit of love, concern themselves with the behaviors that bring serious temporal and eternal consequences. To do anything else—to be more concerned about the names we may be called or the mocking we may receive—would be self-centered.

When Jesus walked the earth, He preached against sin, reminding His listeners that the Law of Moses forbids adultery, anger, murder, divorce, and the like. Yet the crowds didn't shrink—they grew. They grew so large, in fact, that the Pharisees tried to find ways to discredit Jesus so they could rein in His influence.

As I've sought God's guidance, what I've come to realize is that "speaking truth in love" sparks revival. Evangelicals tend to hear "revival" and automatically think back to the Great Awakening or the Billy Graham crusades with nostalgic fondness. Let's stop thinking backward and start praying for God to bring revival in our day.

Sure, there are times when speaking truth in love in the public square is so exhausting and my "enemies" are so hurtful that I consider how much calmer life would be if I lived in the Bible Belt or attended a church where everyone thinks the same way I do. Reality then grabs hold of me, and I'm reminded of Jesus's Great Commission to His followers: "Go therefore and make disciples of all nations, baptizing them in the name of the Father and of the Son and of the Holy Spirit, teaching them to observe all things that I have commanded you" (Matt. 28:19–20, NKJV). To stop evangelizing is to let our neighbors down and ignore the call Christ gave His followers. To stop evangelizing is to live without love for others.

There are many places across the globe where evangelicalism is thriving. Revival is sweeping across Africa, Asia, and Latin America. CBN News reported that an outpouring of Spirit-led voting is changing the political and cultural landscape in many Latin American nations. In this part of the world evangelicals are dedicated to changing the culture, not merging with it. In turn, churches are seeing a tremendous numbers of lives changed. In Brazil, Lagoinha Baptist Church has an astonishing thirty-five thousand members and regularly sees nearly one hundred fifty saved at its Sunday services.[16] Of course, the church's mission is not to draw large numbers. It's to see lives transformed.

The good news is we don't need a big tent full of people to

speak the truth in love that brings transformation. Do you have a child? Attend school? Go to work? Have friends or neighbors? Revival starts in homes and communities before it spreads across nations. With God's help America can experience another great awakening. But first, every one of us must be courageous enough to simply start where we are, sharing the truth of the gospel with those around us because we love them too much not to.

Chapter 11

LIVING OUT BOLD FAITH

> *If you don't say anything, you*
> *can't be called on to repeat it.*[1]
>
> CALVIN COOLIDGE

IN THE MIDST OF THE NATION'S SPIRITUAL DARKNESS, THERE are glimmers of hope. Exceptional young evangelicals are hunched over keyboards and Bibles, working tirelessly to expose distorted theology and reconfigure America's failing moral compass before it's too late.

As we've worked to bridge the divergent values between the generations of evangelicals, I've shared much about my own journey in hopes of alerting you to the strategies of the evangelical Left. But goodness knows that I'm not alone. Now I want to introduce you to other young evangelicals who are sacrificing the world's acceptance and adoration in order to safeguard evangelicalism and share the gospel.

Meet the New Recruits

Stepping outside their comfort zones, these Millennial evangelicals work within the realm of faith, public policy, nonprofits, and the US military. At one point each of them faced a crossroad where progressive, cafeteria-style Christianity and the traditional teachings of Jesus Christ met. They heard the secular and evangelical Left tell them to forgo tradition, determine truth for themselves, and not listen to the "old white guys" encouraging a strong social and political Christian activism. They refused to listen.

Bethany Goodman, assistant director, March for Life Education and Defense Fund, age twenty-eight

What was your childhood church experience like?

My family attended a Methodist church when I was growing up, but it was an evangelical community. But it's funny, if someone would have asked me, "Were you raised in one of those 'hateful' evangelical homes?" I would have responded, "What are you talking about? No, I don't even know what that means." I wasn't aware of the *evangelical* term until college.

Youth group wasn't my thing. I was one of those weird kids because youth group just seemed dumb. I didn't want to play those awkward games. So you could say I rebelled against the youth group mentality of the 1990s. I felt like it wasn't feeding me spiritually. I wasn't finding any of "the answers" there.

Did you have influential mentors growing up?

I had really great Sunday school teachers growing up who taught the entire Bible and talked about having a personal relationship with Jesus. I really loved that. I'm very thankful for my church experience, although my parents were more influential in how I got where I am spiritually.

The first time I learned about abortion was at church. It wasn't an event or sermon; it was just through other individuals talking about abortion. My church did not get into social issues. I really can't remember any type of pro-life talks or events.

But, again, it was really my parents who introduced me to those issues—my dad especially. We would get *World* magazine's kid publication every week. It focused on news stories from a Christian perspective for kids. There was a worksheet attached that you could fill out. So every week our extra homework from Dad was that we had to go through the worksheet and fill it out.

I definitely remember pushing back a little because I didn't want to do the extra homework. But at the same time it gave me a taste for social-interest issues. We also grew up listening to Ravi Zacharias and R. C. Sproul and then to Chuck Colson's *BreakPoint* on the radio. All these things piqued my interest in the news, culture, faith, and history.

Do you ever feel belittled for your faith?

I definitely do. The world thinks we're stupid or ignorant Bible believers. To use my sister as an example, she is a scientist. She has studied molecular biology and received a master's degree in forensic science. Now she is doing cutting-edge DNA research. She is very secure in her beliefs and defense of biblical creation, and yet to the world, her accomplishments would be discounted because of her rejection of evolution.

I feel the same way working for the defense of life. Because I believe in what God's Word says and that abortion has a negative impact on culture, society thinks I'm dumb and that I hate women and children. So defending life is very intimidating some days. But I've found it is even more discouraging when you get pushback from people within the church.

Thankfully, though, because of my faith I have hope and am convinced it's worth it to keep fighting for the truth. Defending the sanctity of life is an issue of justice, human rights, and the flourishing of society.

What is it going to take to strengthen the evangelical community's public witness when it comes to culture and faith?

The church has to talk about these moral issues. Yes, we can keep having sermons that remind us God loves us no matter what, but as soon as we walk out the doors, we are confronted with all these issues. We have to know how to handle them and how to talk about them.

When you look into the future of the church, what do you see?

As I start to think about having a family—goodness, I think things are crazy now, and I can't imagine when my kids are teenagers what the world will look like and what the state of religious liberty will be. It just means we have to keep proclaiming the truth and speaking out for what's best for children, individuals, and culture even as society increasingly embraces abortion, sexual freedom, and the redefinition of marriage. Believers will need to have answers—winsome and grounded in God's Word—to these issues.

Eric Smith, junior officer, United States Navy, age twenty-eight

How did your early church experiences affect your personal relationship with Jesus?

I grew up going to a Baptist church from as early as I can remember. My mother faithfully took us every Sunday, and we used to migrate through numerous vacation Bible schools during the summertime. My dad was not as interested in anything having to do with church or Jesus, but I think he was glad we went nonetheless. I was taught the foundations of faith in Christ through my time in church, and I gave my life to Him when I was nine. One problem in my life, though, was that there seemed to be this separation between my home life and my church life. At church we talked about Jesus and the Bible, but at home not much was said other than, "You better behave."

Did you ever go through a rebellious time or succumb to couch-potato Christianity?

Yes, I did! I would say high school was a wayward time for me and my faith. The main driver for this for me was a lack of male leadership with respect to faith. Again, my dad showed no interest in Jesus, and as I was growing and learning what it meant to be a man, I modeled myself after the men I was around. This only increased the separation between my faith at church and the rest of my life. Internally I was convicted and struggling, and that made me want to hide one part of my life from another.

During this time, did you have a mentor who helped?

The pastor at the church I grew up in always spoke boldly about God's Word, and my heart would be convicted throughout the time I was struggling spiritually. Then when I went to college and there was no longer room to have church and the rest of my life separated, I was at a crossroads. I needed to reconfirm whom I would follow: Christ or myself. I spent a lot of time reading my Bible for the first time in a long time, and I spent my time around friends who were serious about their faith. The Lord never lets go of His children.

Why is it important to you to be bold about your faith?

We are called to be Christ's presence/image bearers in the world. We are called to influence people by word and deed, and our words and deeds should align, lest we be called hypocritical and hurt our witness. If we serve and minister without a voice, then what makes us different from other kindhearted souls who are seeking the betterment of humanity through good works? As we serve, we must proclaim Christ. If all we do is talk with other Christians and sit on the couch, then we are not really in the game. Our life's testimony is the most powerful witness we have. The story of how Christ changed my life—He will do the same for anyone.

What do you think leads to the mind-set that prevents young evangelicals from speaking truth in love?

It is easy to be silent and not "rock the boat," especially to people whose approval you want. Or society tells us it is not loving to tell people things that might make them feel bad or uncomfortable. Or we are scared we don't know what to say and will mess up our attempts to share Christ. When it comes down to it, though, meaningful relationships are not about telling people what they want to hear. They are about being real.

What can young evangelicals expect to face as they speak out boldly for Christ?

They can expect to face skepticism and rejection. Some people will think you're ignorant or narrow-minded while some people may genuinely be curious and open to learning who Jesus is. They can expect to hear arguments that are mixed with bits of truth but are not fully grounded in Scripture. Today the world is filled with the idea that there is a plurality of truths, and truth is whatever the individual wants it to be. Some people will tell you to mind your own business and not force "your values or morals" on others. Jesus was, and is, constantly being rejected by the world, so when we stand and live for Him, we can expect to be treated the same way.

If you could give one piece of encouragement to other evangelicals struggling spiritually, what would that be?

Read your Bible; saturate yourself with the truth. The world is full of lies and smooth talking, and if you don't know how to recognize them, you will be directed whichever way the wind blows. First Peter 3:15 says, "But in your hearts honor Christ the Lord as holy, always being prepared to make a defense to anyone who asks you for a reason for the hope that is in you; yet do it with gentleness and respect." If you are not prepared, how can you tell others the truth so desperately needed in this world?

Alexandria Palazzo, congressional lobbyist, age twenty-four

Did you ever go through a rebellious time or, perhaps, buy into cafeteria-style Christianity?

Yes. As a result of my parents' divorce, I began to question foundational principles that I had believed since childhood. I chose to transfer to Liberty University in hopes of getting sound guidance and knowledge on biblical principles.

During this time did you have a mentor who helped you ground your faith?

My aunt. During difficult times in my life she has always provided me with godly wisdom and encouragement.

Did you ever go through a period when you hesitated to engage in the culture wars?

Yes. Growing up in upstate New York, finding a strong conservative was a rarity. When I did, they weren't politically engaged, nor did anyone teach us how to speak on biblical issues facing society. During my freshman year in college, I was attending Buffalo State University, and I found myself faced with the issue of abortion. I knew abortion was wrong, but I didn't know how to tell that to my friend, who wasn't a Christian. Not being able to express why abortion was wrong and the inability to encourage my friend to seek other options led me to seek out answers so I could better engage culture-war issues.

Have you ever felt intimidated or ostracized for defending your Christian convictions?

I have felt intimidated to express my Christian values and convictions. But the more I spoke out, the more comfortable I became with expressing my views. It also helps to have a theme song. No joke! Mine is "Courageous" by Casting Crowns.

What do you think prevents some young evangelicals from speaking truth in love?

I think many young evangelicals feel outnumbered. Society and culture tell them if they aren't "accepting" of progressive views, then they are being an extremist. To a young person today, being an extremist is a very negative thing. Our society is all about emotion, and as Christians we strive to live a disciplined, moderate life, not one fueled by passion. It's difficult to find the middle ground of speaking out in love and holding your principles.

If you could give fellow young evangelicals one piece of advice or encouragement, what would that be?

You aren't alone. You have people who agree with you. Keep in mind that you were called for just a time as this. If history has taught us anything, it's that it takes courage to speak out and stand up for your principles, but that didn't stop our Founding Fathers and that shouldn't stop you. Find your courage in knowledge; the more you understand how to speak about your principles, the less people will be able to discourage you.

Eric Teetsel, executive director, the Manhattan Declaration, age thirty

Since you grew up in a military family, what was your church experience like?

My parents are both Christians. My dad was in the army, so we moved all throughout my childhood. Every time we moved, we would just sort of pick a church. I'm not really sure what drove my parents to pick one over the other. When we were overseas, we always went to the military chapels, which tended to be very conservative but generically Protestant.

It wasn't until I went to Wheaton College that I even realized how deep denomination roots go for many people and was exposed to the fact that these eighteen-year-olds had very firm opinions about eschatology and all kinds of random, tertiary theological issues. Suffice it to say, Wheaton was a real growth experience for me. I was a believer going in, but I knew when I was choosing a college that if I went to the University of Arizona instead of Wheaton I wouldn't be built up as the kind of Christian man I needed to be.

When you graduated from high school, did you intend to be a culture warrior?

No, I didn't. I didn't even know what I wanted to study. I had always been interested in politics in high school. I remember once in high school asking my dad, "Do you think it's possible to be a Democrat and a Christian?" He sort of slapped me down and said, "Of course it is." But I wrestled with that question, and I think I still wrestle with that question. I studied political science for a time. Eventually I landed on communications. Then I decided to go into Christian higher education at the encouraging of a mentor of mine.

So I went to Azusa Pacific University and started in a master's program in college student affairs, assuming that if I went to another evangelical institution I would be prepared to do Christ-centered higher education with all the distinctions that should make it different from any other education experience.

Did attending an evangelical university help you develop a strong Christian worldview?

Unfortunately, my experience at Azusa was quite disappointing. I found that it was Christian only in the sense that we would do a devotional before class and then immediately jump into the same material they were studying at USC [University of Southern California] down the street, including all of the tolerance, pro-gay, white guilt stuff. In fact, I would say that was the majority of what we learned. Until that point in graduate school, I had forgotten about politics and conservatism. It wasn't my thing. I wasn't studying it. I was more interested in girls and intramural sports. In graduate school those interests were rekindled because I was looking around going, "This isn't Christian. There is nothing distinctive about this. We are not focused on putting Christ first and then exploring the demands He puts on how we live and what we think." That is not a question that anyone was asking.

What was your "crossroads" moment?

For me everything came to a head in a class on diversity and tolerance. A guest speaker was brought in to talk about how we should work with students struggling with same-sex identity issues. I was really excited to hear him because this is a common experience among college students, especially on a Christian campus. So we need to be equipped to handle it. Instead, the guest speaker said the reason these students are in crisis is because we keep telling them these things are wrong. And if we would just allow them to embrace who they are, we wouldn't have these problems.

So after listening for a while, I finally raised my hand and said, "Wouldn't you agree that even if you dismiss some of the specific verses that speak to homosexuality that there is a broader theology of human sexuality that goes from Genesis to Revelation that affirms heterosexuality?" And he said, "No, I don't agree, and I would invite you to stop speaking." I was trying to have a conversation about these things and instead I was silenced and dismissed.

Later I started going to conferences like the Association for Christians in Student Development conference and saw a regurgitation of mainstream ideological garbage. It left me wondering, "How are we allowing this to affect Christ-centered institutions of higher education?" We have to do better than this.

How is liberation theology managing to take root on evangelical campuses?

I think it all boils down to the monopoly that graduate school programs have on shaping future educators. You have a limited crop of PhD programs available. You get into a program and are surrounded by people who generally think the same, which is often contrary to what we believe. Imagine that your graduate assistantship, scholarships, and future as an academic are all riding on what your colleagues think about you. In order to survive that environment, you have to pretend you believe the one side of the issue. There is no accountability. If you don't toe the line, you can spend five years doing all the work and at the end be denied a degree.

When did you decide to step into the faith and public policy arena full time?

At twenty-seven, Timothy Goeglein at Focus on the Family told me the Manhattan Declaration was looking to hire their first and only employee. I think my response was, "That still exists?" I applied, and Chuck Colson interviewed me over the phone. And then I was offered the job. I started in April of 2012, and Chuck died a week before I started. He was the impetus behind starting the Manhattan Declaration and hiring someone to carry on the defense of life, liberty, and marriage in culture.

So it was as if Chuck Colson passed the torch on to you?

In a way he did. It's incredible to think about how in 2009 he was thinking about life, marriage, and religious freedom. These weren't the issues the American people were talking about back then. It was the wars in Iraq and Afghanistan, the economy, and health care reform. And yet he had a sense of them before these three issues came to the floor. And, wow, look where we are today.

The Manhattan Declaration focuses on issues at the forefront of American life, but it is deep and philosophical and can be inaccessible. So what we aim to do is break down the issues for everyday Christians so they can be effective influencers in their communities.

Jessica Prol, public policy editor, Family Research Council, age thirty-one

Why did you decide to work in faith and public policy?

Honestly, I came to Washington DC to try and change the world. That's been an awkward, laughable thing. But I have seen some of the mechanisms of change and with that a growing appreciation for the church of God.

I quickly began to integrate myself into Capitol Hill Baptist Church, which is in friendly cooperation with the Southern Baptist Convention. It was a strong fit for me intellectually, and it had warmth that I hadn't seen modeled in many other churches I had experienced over the years.

How might an evangelical Christian "change the world"?

I've recognized other avenues for cultural change in civil society beyond political activism. Teachers shape tomorrow's leaders and change the world through education. The films we produce and books we write are all ways to change hearts and minds, not simply the legislation we pass.

I am pursuing a counseling degree part-time at Westminster Theological Seminary. I'm pursuing that for a variety of reasons. I've been blessed to see a Christian counseling movement emerge that is thoroughly biblical but sensitive. I see it emerging, and that's been a really helpful addition to my spiritual journey. Unlike some of my peers, I haven't been crazy scarred by the church, but it is comforting to see greater depth and more compassion than I've seen in other circles. I've also been near enough to tragic circumstances to I know I want more wisdom.

I've also wanted to pursue counseling because we in the social policy world are talking about issues that are intimate, personal, and deep. Even when we are relying on social science data, we're smack-dab in the middle of people's most private and intimate business. We're saying that certain kinds of sexual behavior are broken and harmful. This can be hurtful and offensive. I don't believe that's reason enough to keep our mouths shut. After all, adult sexuality has serious implications on society and children. But I want to learn how to talk about these explosive topics in a gentle, compassionate, and very sensitive, personal way. For me, that means keeping a foot in public writing and speaking while also gaining expertise in private ministry.

In light of pursuing counseling, do you still consider yourself a culture warrior?

I still have this persistent itch to be engaged in the public discussion. And so by your definition, yes, I am sort of reluctantly labeling myself a culture warrior, reluctantly because of the baggage the label carries. But I also sense that calling because there are very direct attacks on the institution of marriage and some pretty persistent lies about what it means to be human.

At Family Research Council we don't just talk about gay marriage and abortion. We also talk about adoption and human trafficking. Those are not squishy or soft issues. But my goal is to explain why human trafficking is wrong. I think it is directly tied to the idea of sexuality that we have thoroughly messed up.

I haven't always felt comfortable with these "culture war" issues. I remember shortly before I moved to DC, I was at the Leadership Institute for a communications class. I remember hearing a conservative and a libertarian duke it out over gay marriage. I didn't want to be involved. I remember thinking, "Oh, I hope I never have to weigh in on these sorts of issues." Now here I am a decade later, and these issues are not going away. Some days I'd rather not be fighting. But our culture's lies about freedom and sexuality are costing human lives. Because I care so deeply, it's not time for me to pull out. That's why I'm still here.

What trends—positive or negative—do you see playing out in faith and culture?

I'm concerned by the way our country and especially my peers value sexual freedom and expression over freedom of conscience. The word *bigot* is thrown around so easily, with little logic or concern for orthodox Christian belief about human sexuality. I expect this problem to get worse before it gets better.

However, I'm encouraged to see our country trending in a pro-life direction. We've seen numerous, recent laws enacted to protect unborn life. But I think this legislative progress has been possible largely due to personal, sensitive ministry to women in crisis and greater awareness about the emotional and physical costs of abortion—both to the baby and to the mother. I'm praying and working toward telling a more compelling narrative in other areas of social policy—beyond abortion. Our Savior has promised us that the truth would set us free. I think that verse applies to truth even about human sexuality. I wouldn't be doing this work if I didn't think that promise would hold up under pressure.

Joseph Rossell, policy analyst and producer for CDR Communications, age twenty-four

How did having Christian parents shape your faith?

I grew up in a Christian home, but, of course, this doesn't mean I was born a Christian. As I got older—during my late elementary years and into early middle school—I began asking questions about my faith. I needed to rationalize what I'd heard from my parents and church my whole life and decide whether I believed the tenets of Christianity for myself.

Did you go through a rebellious stage as a teenager?

I never really "acted out," but I had to deal with things every kid does, like conflict with my siblings and obeying my parents.

It wasn't until I'd thought through and accepted the Christian faith as my own that my heart changed and my behavior toward those around me improved. So, for me, the progression of change in my life was very much first mind, second heart, and finally actions.

How did you get involved in the culture wars?

I'd have a tough time pinpointing any particular event or experience that led me to the culture wars. I believe each step in my personal journey from the very beginning has led me deeper into the war zone and brought me closer to God's will for my life.

I've had an interest in public policy for as long as I can remember. Current events and politics captured my attention from a young age. I remember following the election cycle, reading the newspaper, and watching the evening news from at least the age of nine or ten—probably sooner.

I also have a creative side that has shaped how I relate to the culture. We have family photos of me plunking away at the piano as a toddler, a passion (and skill) that has developed over a couple of decades now. In high school and college I also took an interest in writing and multimedia. Both of these passions I was able to develop in college and apply professionally.

Each organization I've been privileged to work for has advocated a mission that runs in tandem with my beliefs. Each has supported public policy interests and some facet of my creative side to advance issues relating to my Christian faith.

What culture issues tug at your heartstrings the most?

I couldn't agree more with author Julian Simon than when he wrote that human beings are the "most important of all" resources.[2] Because I believe passionately that God created man in His own image and that we are all wonderfully and fearfully made, I am also passionately pro-life, pro-immigration, and pro-economic development. I believe that humans should exert responsible dominion over God's creation and that governments should protect the rights of people. I want to see women receive the same rights around the world as men; I want children (both boys and girls) to get the best education available so they can achieve their fullest potential. Those are just a few of the issues I care the most about, all of which are an outflow of God's valuation of human beings.

Did you ever go through a period when you hesitated to engage in the culture wars?

Yes. One group I worked with took a stand in the cultural battle over the environment. A lot of extremists on the other side didn't like what we said, and we received plenty of hate. I found it intimidating, but also defining. It prompted me to reconsider my commitment to the issues I think are important. I ultimately came to the conclusion that no matter the costs, I need to stick to and advocate for what I believe in with boldness. It also taught me to trust God for my safety; He will protect me from anyone who hates me or wishes me harm for as long as He wills. My days are in His hand.

What do you think stops young evangelical from speaking truth in love?

I think very few young evangelicals relate to the world with an attitude of "humble orthodoxy."[3] I first heard this phrase from author and speaker Josh Harris, and I find it helpfully describes the two directions through which young evangelicals tend to veer off track.

Many get the "humble" part or the "orthodoxy" part right, but rarely both at the same time. It can be so easy either to assert your dogmas self-righteously or bend meekly to the world's ideology. The proper balance is neither stubborn arrogance nor misguided diffidence in the face of opposition, but a firm (though humble) commitment to our core beliefs.

Our goal should be to emulate Martin Luther as he stood before the Diet of Worms in April 1521. After much thoughtful introspection, Luther spoke boldly to the powerful body in front of which he had been interrogated the day before:

> Unless I am convinced by the testimony of the Scriptures or by clear reason (for I do not trust either in the pope or in councils alone, since it is well known that they have often erred and contradicted themselves), I am bound by the Scriptures I have quoted, and my conscience is captive to the word of God. I cannot and I will not recant anything, since it is neither safe nor right to go against conscience. May God help me. Amen.[4]

Luther was willing to listen to logic; he was open to sound scriptural reasoning. But he wouldn't budge from his convictions if he wasn't convinced. So he held his ground—not in a flashy or confrontational way, but humbly.

At the end of the day, what's it going to take to save evangelicalism?

Revival. Specifically, it's going to take God working powerfully through His Spirit in the hearts of Christians and unbelievers alike, drawing us to take part in His glorious kingdom purposes. I think that we need to pray for God to grant us opportunities to express His truth, properly seasoned words for our times, and the boldness to speak even when it's hard. Ultimately, we aren't going to produce cultural change. Only God will. We need His miraculous power to changes hearts and minds.

Footprints to Follow

Evangelicals do not have to move to Washington DC to "change the world." The young evangelicals who shared their stories had one common thread—they are simply *willing* to follow God's calling on their lives.

Consider the story about Jesus feeding the five thousand in John 6. To make an important point, Jesus asked His disciple Philip where he could find enough food to feed the huge crowd that kept following Him. Philip's answer was full of doubt. He said, "Even if we worked for months, we wouldn't have enough money to feed them!" (v. 7, NLT).

In your mind you're probably skipping to the end of the story, because you know what happens. Jesus multiplies a kid-size lunch of five loaves of bread and two fish into king-size portions.

Step back for a moment, though, and think about the little boy whose meager lunch was used by God. A youngster with only cheap bread and small fish offered up what little he had when the grown-up disciples backed down in doubt. And because of this child's willingness, Jesus fed the five thousand both physically and spiritually.

For change to happen, every one of us has to be willing to show up and influence the world around us. We have to be willing to offer our resources, our talents, and our positions of influence in our families, churches, and government. We must be willing to share the gospel without reservation. Willing to be mocked. Willing to be ostracized. Willing to experience the worst.

Ronald Reagan once said that freedom is never "more than one generation away from extinction. It is not ours by inheritance; it must be fought for and defended constantly by each generation, for it comes only once to a people."[5]

The same is true with faith. We must wrestle to shine a light on truth and equip and empower the next generation of evangelicals to avoid lethargic evangelicalism. However, we must also realize that we are mere mortals and know when to step aside.

Our heavenly Father is the ultimate role model. One of my own mentors once told me, "Good evangelism goes something like this: Be faithful, show up, know God's story, know your story, yield to the Holy Spirit, and deliver the message. Then the person gets convicted, seeks God, and is saved."

Saving evangelicalism will not be easy. It boils down to arming ourselves with Scripture, prayer, and courage; keeping our compassion yet never compromising our convictions; and representing Christ even when it's inconvenient and costly. This is a great challenge. But it is one we must pray every generation of evangelicals is willing to take on for Jesus Christ.

The church itself is facing a crossroads. First Peter 3:15 instructs, "But in your hearts honor Christ the Lord as holy, always being prepared to make a defense to anyone who asks you for a reason for the hope that is in you; yet do it with gentleness and respect." For too long evangelicals have been so focused on threats launched from secular society that we neglected the erosion occurring within our own sanctuaries. It's time to refocus our trajectory. It is time to start defending the reason for our hope within our churches, seminaries, and, for some, our own homes.

It is worth the battle. America needs us. The church needs you.

NOTES

Chapter 1
Facing the Problem

1. Dorothy Sayers, "Creed or Chaos?", May 4, 1940, http://douglassocialcredit.com/Sayers%20Dorothy%20L%20Creed%20or%20Chaos.pdf (accessed May 13, 2014).

2. Pew Research Center, "Changes in Americans' Religious Affiliation," http://www.pewforum.org/2008/02/01/chapter-2-changes-in-americans-religious-affiliation/ (accessed May 13, 2014).

3. Ibid.

4. Marty King, "Number of SBC Churches Increased Last Year; Members, Attendance, and Baptisms Declined," LifeWay, http://www.lifeway.com/Article/news-2012-southern-baptist-annual-church-profile-report (accessed May 13, 2014).

5. Libby Lovelace, "LifeWay Research Finds the New Church View of Young Adults," LifeWay, http://www.lifeway.com/Article/LifeWay-Research-finds-the-new-church-view-of-young-adults (accessed May 13, 2014).

6. T. C. Pinckney, "We Are Losing Our Children," Alliance for the Separation of School and State, http://www.schoolandstate.org/SBC/Pinckney-WeAreLosingOurChildren.htm (accessed May 13, 2014).

7. Lovelace, "LifeWay Research Finds the New Church View of Young Adults."

8. Dietrich Bonhoeffer, *The Cost of Discipleship* (New York: Simon & Schuster, 1995), 44–45.

9. Jon Nielson, "Why Youth Stay in the Church When They Grow Up," Church Leaders, http://www.churchleaders.com/youth/youth-leaders-articles/153948-why-youth-stay-in-the-church-when-they-grow-up.html (accessed May 20, 2014).

10. Matt K. Lewis, "The Culture War Was Never a Fair Fight," *The Week*, March 27, 2013, http://theweek.com/article/index/241871/the-culture-war-was-never-a-fair-fight (accessed May 20, 2014).

11. Pascal-Emmanuel Gobry, "Here's the Simple Reason Why the Religious Right Isn't Finished," *Forbes*, January 23, 2014, http://www.forbes.com/sites/pascalemmanuelgobry/2014/01/23/heres-the-simple-reason-why-the-religious-right-isnt-finished/ (accessed May 20, 2014).

12. Frank Newport, *God Is Alive and Well: The Future of Religion in America* (New York: Gallup Press, 2012), 44.

13. Edmund W. Robb and Julia Robb, *The Betrayal of the Church: Apostasy & Renewal in the Mainline Denominations* (Wheaton, IL: Crossway Books, 1986), 12.

14. Alan Wisdom, ed., "Television Ads Fail to Revive Mainline Denominations," *Faith and Freedom* 25, no. 4 (Fall/Winter 2006): 4.

15. Mark Tooley, *Taking Back the United Methodist Church* (Fort Valley, GA: Bristol House, 2008) 178.

16. Lewis Andrews, "School Choice and the Mainline Protestant Future," *Faith and Freedom* 24, no. 3 (Summer 2005): 18–20.

17. Erik Eckholm, "Even on Religious Campuses, Students Fight for Gay Identity," *New York Times*, April 18, 2011, http://www.nytimes.com/2011/04/19/us/19gays.html?_r=0 (accessed May 20, 2014).

18. A. W. Tozer, *Tozer on Christian Leadership* (Camp Hill, PA: Wingspread Publishers, 2007).

Chapter 2
When Faith Meets Culture

1. As quoted in M. Sears, *The American Politician* (Boston: E. Leland and W. J. Whiting, 1842), 139.

2. Wendy Wright, "Why More Than Ever We Must Be Involved," Concerned Women for America, http://www.cwfa.org/wp-content/uploads/2013/11/morethanever.pdf (accessed May 20, 2014).

3. Steve Deace, "Lies & Clever Myths," Townhall.com, January 19, 2013, http://townhall.com/columnists/stevedeace/2013/01/19/lies--clever-myths-n1490861 (accessed May 20, 2014).

4. Jill Stanek, "Links to Barack Obama's Votes on Illinois' Born Alive Infant Protection Act," *JillStanek.com* (blog), February 19, 2008, http://www.jillstanek.com/2008/02/links-to-barack-obamas-votes-on-illinois-born-alive-infant-protection-act/ (accessed May 20, 2014).

5. James Madison, "Proclamation 20—Recommending a Day of Public Thanksgiving for Peace," March 4, 1815, http://www.presidency.ucsb.edu/ws/?pid=65984 (accessed May 20, 2014).

6. Penny Young Nance, "When Picking a President, I Still Believe That Character Counts," Fox News, December 2, 2011, http://www.foxnews.com/opinion/2011/12/02/when-picking-president-still-believe-that-character-counts/ (accessed May 20, 2014).

7. Kevin Robillard, "Election 2012: Study: Youth Vote Was Decisive," Politco.com, November 7, 2012, http://www.politico.com/news/stories/1112/83510.html (accessed May 20, 2014); The Center for Information and Research on Civic Learning and Engagement, "At Least 80 Electoral Votes Depend on Youth," http://www.civicyouth.org/at-least-80-electoral-votes-depended-on-youth/ (accessed May 20, 2014).

8. The George Washington Society, "The Faith and Wisdom of George Washington," http://www.georgewashingtonsociety.org/Mission.html (accessed May 20, 2014).

9. Dale Hudson, "Katy Perry and Why Pastors' Kids Fall Away," Charisma News, http://www.charismanews.com/opinion/42788-katy-perry -and-why-pastor-s-kids-fall-away (accessed May 20, 2014);

10. Barna Group, "Prodigal Pastor Kids: Fact or Fiction," https://www .barna.org/barna-update/family-kids/644-prodigal-pastor-kids-fact-or -fiction#.Uv4bGF5kIhx (accessed May 20, 2014).

11. Todd Starnes, "American Humanist Association Sues Teacher Who Prayed for Sick Student," Fox News, November 26, 2013, http://www .foxnews.com/opinion/2013/11/26/american-humanist-association-sues -teacher-who-prayed-for-sick-student/ (accessed May 20, 2014).

12. WFMZ-TV News, "Teacher Fired Over Bible Files Compliant Against Phillipsburg School District," April 15, 2013, http://www.wfmz .com/news/news-regional-newjersey/Teacher-fired-over-Bible-files -complaint-against-Phillipsburg-School-District/-/132518/19713834/-/ 1489h0y/-/index.html (accessed May 20, 2014).

13. Don Byrd, "High School Coach Agrees to Stop Leading Prayer, Proselytizing Team," Baptist Joint Committee for Religious Liberty, February 4, 2014, http://www.bjconline.org/index.php?option=com_content &task=view&id=5873&Itemid=134 (accessed May 20, 2014), emphasis added.

14. Daniel L. Dreisbach, "The Mythical 'Wall of Separation': How a Misused Metaphor Changed Church-State Law, Policy, and Discourse," The Heritage Foundation, June 23, 2006, http://www.heritage.org/ research/reports/2006/06/the-mythical-wall-of-separation-how-a -misused-metaphor-changed-church-state-law-policy-and-discourse (accessed May 20, 2014).

15. Thinkexist.com, "Patrick Henry Quotes," http://en.thinkexist.com/ quotation/bad_men_cannot_make_good_citizens-it_is/154033 .html (accessed May 20, 2014).

16. ABC News, "Read the Transcript of Ashcroft's Speech at Bob Jones U.," http://abcnews.go.com/Politics/story?id=122064 (accessed May 20, 2014).

17. National Archives, "Declaration of Independence," http://www .archives.gov/exhibits/charters/declaration_transcript.html (accessed May 20, 2014).

18. Library of Congress, "Religion and the Founding of the American Republic," http://www.loc.gov/exhibits/religion/rel06.html (accessed May 20, 2014).

19. Mario Diaz, "Self-Evident Truths, Part IV: Remember the Sabbath," Concerned Women for America, August 9, 2011, http://www.cwfa

.org/self-evident-truths-part-iv-remember-the-sabbath/ (accessed May 20, 2014).

20. BBC News, "North Korea Confirms US Citizen Is Arrested," April 14, 2011, http://www.bbc.co.uk/news/world-asia-pacific-13075699 (accessed May 20, 2014).

21. US Department of State, "International Religious Freedom Report 2003," http://www.state.gov/j/drl/rls/irf/2003/24449.htm (accessed May 20, 2014).

22. Ronald R. Cherry, "Judeo-Christian Values," *American Thinker*, October 6, 2007, http://www.americanthinker.com/2007/10/judeochristian_values.html (accessed May 20, 2014).

23. John J. Pitney Jr., "The Tocqueville Fraud," *Weekly Standard*, November 13, 1995, http://www.tocqueville.org/pitney.htm (accessed May 20, 2014).

24. Ronald Reagan, "Inaugural Address, January 5, 1967," *The Public Papers of President Ronald W. Reagan*, Ronald Reagan Presidential Library, http://www.reagan.utexas.edu/archives/speeches/govspeech/01051967a.htm (accessed June 25, 2014).

Chapter 3
Emerging From the Emergent Movement

1. Goodreads.com, "G. K. Chesterton Quotes," https://www.goodreads.com/quotes/599983-don-t-ever-take-a-fence-down-until-you-know-the (accessed May 20, 2014).

2. Walter A. Elwell, ed., *Evangelical Dictionary of Theology* (Grand Rapids, MI: Baker Book House, 1984), 381.

3. Ibid.

4. Richard Quebedeaux, *The Young Evangelicals: The Revolution in Orthodoxy* (New York: Harper & Row, 1974), 28–37.

5. C-Span, "Women and the Conservative Movement," *Washington Journal*, August 29, 2011, http://www.c-span.org/video/?301255-3/WomenandtheCo (accessed May 20, 2014).

6. Ross Douthat, *Bad Religion: How We Became a Nation of Heretics* (New York: Free Press, 2012), 3.

7. Sojourners, "Mission Statement," http://sojo.net/about-us/mission-statement (accessed May 10, 2014).

8. As quoted in David P. Gushee, ed., *A New Evangelical Manifesto* (St. Louis, MO: Chalice Press, 2012), 31.

9. Rachel Held Evans, "Why Millennials Are Leaving the Church," CNN.com, July 27, 2013, http://religion.blogs.cnn.com/2013/07/27/why-millennials-are-leaving-the-church/ (accessed May 20, 2014).

10. Chelsen Vicari, "Why Liberal Evangelicals are Lying to Millennials," TheBlaze, October 5, 2013, http://www.theblaze.com/

contributions/why-liberal-evangelicals-are-lying-to-millennials/ (accessed May 21, 2014).

11. Marvin Olasky, "Jim Wallis vs. The Truth," *World Magazine*, August 18, 2010, http://www.worldmag.com/2010/08/jim_wallis_vs_the_truth (accessed May 21, 2014); Billy Hallowell, "Jim Wallis' Ultra-Lib Christian Mag 'Sojourners' Has Ties to Soros, Democratic Ideals," TheBlaze, July 13, 2011, http://www.theblaze.com/stories/2011/07/13/jim-wallis-ultra-lib-christian-mag-sojourners-has-ties-to-soros-democratic-ideals/ (accessed May 21, 2014); Dave Urbanski, "George Soros Sends $150,000 to Jim Wallis' Left-Wing Group Sojourners," TheBlaze, October 10, 2011, http://www.theblaze.com/stories/2011/10/12/george-soros-sends-150000-to-jim-wallis-left-wing-christian-magazine/ (accessed May 21, 2014).

12. Joe Wolverton II, "Soros Promotes UN Control Over Gun Ownership," *The New American*, http://www.thenewamerican.com/usnews/constitution/item/11983-soros-promotes-un-control-over-gun-ownership (accessed May 21, 2014); Alexander H. Joffe, "Bad Investment: The Philanthropy of George Soros and the Arab-Israeli Conflict," NGO Monitor, May 2013, http://www.ngo-monitor.org/soros.pdf (accessed May 21, 2014).

13. Sarah Pulliam Bailey, "Wallis Apologizes to Olasky after Sojourners Funding Flap," *Christianity Today*, August 26, 2010, http://www.christianitytoday.com/ct/2010/augustweb-only/44-41.0.html (accessed May 21, 2014).

14. Roger Wolsey, "16 Ways Progressive Christians Interpret the Bible," Patheos, January 14, 2014, http://www.patheos.com/blogs/rogerwolsey/2014/01/16-ways-progressive-christians-interpret-the-bible/ (accessed May 21, 2014).

15. Brian D. McLaren, *A New Kind of Christianity: Ten Questions That Are Transforming the Faith* (New York: HarperCollins, 2010), 7.

16. The Lutheran Church—Missouri Synod, "The Emergent Church, an Evaluation From the Theological Perspective of the Lutheran Church—Missouri Synod," January 2011, http://www.lcms.org/page.aspx?pid=695 (accessed May 20, 2014).

17. Adam Smith, "The End of the Emergent Movement?", *Relevant Magazine*, April 12, 2010, http://www.relevantmagazine.com/god/church/features/21181-the-end-of-emergent (accessed May 21, 2014).

18. The Lutheran Church—Missouri Synod, "The Emergent Church, an Evaluation From the Theological Perspective of the Lutheran Church—Missouri Synod."

19. Smith, "The End of the Emergent Movement?"

20. Ibid.

21. John Piper, "What Is the 'Emerging Church,'" DesiringGod.org, March 12, 2008, http://www.desiringgod.org/interviews/what-is-the -emerging-church (accessed May 21, 2014).

22. "Cohorts," *Emergent Village*, http://emergentvillage.org/newev/ ?page_id=29 (accessed May 13, 2014).

23. Stephanie Samuel, "Evangelical Left Leader: Social Justice Is Biblical, 'Pretty Conservative,'" *Christian Post*, March 10, 2011, http://m .christianpost.com/news/evangelical-left-leader-social-justice-is-biblical -pretty-conservative-49358/ (accessed May 22, 2014).

24. Rebecca Lee, "Punk Pastor Preaches Tolerance, Compassion," ABC News, December 8, 2006, http://abcnews.go.com/WNT/Story?id =2711472&page=2 (accessed May 22, 2014).

25. Kristin Rudolph, "Jay Bakker's Rainbow Bread 'Communion,'" *Juicy Ecumenism* (blog), The Institute on Religion & Democracy, May 15, 2013, http://juicyecumenism.com/2013/05/15/jay-bakkers-rainbow-bread -communion/ (accessed May 22, 2014); Jay Bakker, "Vulgar Grace Throws the First Stone" (sermon), May 12, 2013, http://www.revolutionchurch .com/vulgar-grace-throws-the-first-stone/ (accessed May 22, 2014).

26. Kelefa Sanneh, "The Hell-Raiser," *New Yorker*, November 26, 2012, http://www.newyorker.com/reporting/2012/11/26/121126fa_fact_ sanneh?currentPage=all&pink=j8D8IQ (accessed May 22, 2014).

27. Charles Honey, "'Velvet Elvis' Author Encourages Exploration of Doubts," Beliefnet, http://www.beliefnet.com/Faiths/Christianity/ 2005/08/Velvet-Elvis-Author-Encourages-Exploration-Of-Doubts .aspx?p=2 (accessed May 22, 2014).

28. Rob Bell, *Velvet Elvis* (Grand Rapids, MI: Zondervan, 2005), 74.

29. Nicola Menzie, "Rob Bell to Join Oprah Winfrey, Other Handpicked Thought Leaders for 'Life You Want' Tour," *Christian Post*, March 27, 2014, http://www.christianpost.com/news/rob-bell-to-join-oprah -winfrey-other-handpicked-thought-leaders-for-life-you-want-tour-116902/ (accessed May 22, 2014).

30. Chelsen Vicari, "Meet the New 'Punk' Powerhouse of the Emergent Movement," *Juicy Ecumenism* (blog), The Institute on Religion & Democracy, November 7, 2013, http://juicyecumenism.com/2013/11/07/ meet-liberal-evangelicals-rising-star/ (accessed May 22, 2014).

31. Sarah Pulliam Bailey, "Tony Campolo to Shutter His 40-Year-Old Ministry," *Christian Century*, January 14, 2014, http://www .christiancentury.org/article/2014-01/tony-campolo-shutter-evangelical -ministry-he-started-40-years-ago (accessed May 22, 2014).

32. Jonathan Merritt, "Tony Campolo Hits Hard on Abortion, Gay Marriage, Israel and More," Religion News Service, December 17, 2013, http://jonathanmerritt.religionnews.com/2013/12/17/tony-campolo-hits -hard-hot-button-issues/ (accessed May 22, 2014).

33. Mark Caplin, "Tony Campolo: Obama Should Meet Kim Jong-un," *Christian Today*, April 6, 2013, http://www.christiantoday.com/article/ tony.campolo.obama.should.meet.kim.jong.un/32054.htm (accessed May 22, 2014).

34. Tony Campolo, "A Possible Compromise on the Gay Marriage Controversy," Huffington Post, http://www.huffingtonpost.com/tony -campolo/a-possible-compromise-on-_b_826170.html (accessed May 22, 2014).

35. Richard Cizik, "My Journey Toward the 'New Evangelicalism,'" ReligionandPolitics.org, September 13, 2012, http://religionandpolitics .org/2012/09/13/my-journey-toward-the-new-evangelicalism/ (accessed May 22, 2014).

36. Shane Claiborne, *The Irresistible Revolution* (Grand Rapids, MI: Zondervan, 2006) 23.

37. Ibid., 250, emphasis added.

38. Ibid., 157.

39. Jennifer D. Crumpton, "The Worst Lie of Election 2012: Women Are 'Shiny Objects' of 'Distraction,'" *Femmevangelical* (blog), Patheos, October 29, 2012, http://www.patheos.com/blogs/femmevangelical/ 2012/10/the-worst-lie-of-election-2012-women-are-shiny-objects-of -distraction/ (accessed May 22, 2014).

40. Brittney R. Villalva, "Woman Living Biblically for One Year Writes Book: Rachel Evans' Life-Changing Experience," *Christian Post*, October 18, 2012, http://www.christianpost.com/news/woman-living-biblically -for-one-year-writes-book-rachel-evans-life-changing-experience-photo -83515/ (accessed May 22, 2014).

41. Kathy Keller, "Rachel Held Evans," The Gospel Coalition, http:// legacy.thegospelcoalition.org/themelios/review/a_year_of_biblical_ womanhood (accessed May 22, 2014).

42. Rachel Held Evans, "Privilege and the Pill," *RachelHeldEvans.com* (blog), http://rachelheldevans.com/blog/privilege-and-the-pill (accessed May 22, 2014).

43. Lynne Hybels, "The Israeli-Palestinian Conflict: Six Things I Believe," *lynnehybels* (blog), http://lynnehybels.blogspot.com/2013/12/the -israeli-palestinian-conflict-six.html (accessed May 22, 2014).

44. Tony Jones, "Let's Talk About What Happened Yesterday," *Theo- blogy* (blog), Patheos, March 27, 2014, http://www.patheos.com/blogs/ tonyjones/2014/03/27/lets-talk-about-what-happened-yesterday-at-world -vision/ (accessed May 22, 2014).

45. Tony Jones, What's a Christian to Do With…Dan Savage?", *Theo- blogy* (blog), Patheos, July 11, 2011, http://www.patheos.com/blogs/ tonyjones/2011/07/11/whats-a-christian-to-do-with-dan-savage/ (accessed May 22, 2014).

46. Tony Jones, "Is It Time for Christians to Celebrate Pre-Marital Sex?", *Theoblogy* (blog), Patheos, February 6, 2013, http://www.patheos.com/blogs/tonyjones/2013/02/06/is-it-time-for-christians-to-celebrate-pre-marital-sex/ (accessed May 22, 2014).

47. Chelsen Vicari, "What Brian McLaren Can Learn From Mark Driscoll," *Juicy Ecumenism* (blog), The Institute on Religion & Democracy, October 22, 2013, http://juicyecumenism.com/2013/10/22/what-brian-mclaren-can-learn-from-mark-driscoll/ (accessed May 22, 2014).

48. Brian McLaren, "Q & R: Are You a Universalist? Or a Whig?" *Brian D. Mclaren* (blog), http://brianmclaren.net/archives/blog/after-reading-why-did-jesus.html (accessed June 10, 2014).

49. Audrey Barrick, "Brian McLaren's Son Marries Same-Sex Partner," *Christian Post*, September 25, 2012, http://www.christianpost.com/news/brian-mclarens-son-marries-same-sex-partner-82209/ (accessed May 22, 2014).

50. Chelsen Vicari, "The Real Christian Conference Conundrum," *Juicy Ecumenism* (blog), The Institute on Religion & Democracy, December 19, 2013, http://juicyecumenism.com/2013/12/19/the-real-christian-conference-conundrum/ (accessed May 22, 2014); *Simply Jesus: (re)Discovering the Ways of Jesus*, DVD, www.simplyjesusgathering.com.

51. Vicari, "The Real Christian Conference Conundrum."

52. Kristin Rudolph, "Jim Wallis: Government Should Make Life Fair," *Juicy Ecumenism* (blog), The Institute on Religion & Democracy, April 9, 2013, http://juicyecumenism.com/2013/04/09/jim-wallis-government-should-make-life-fair/ (accessed May 22, 2014).

53. Ted Olsen, "Where Jim Wallis Stands," *Christianity Today*, April 16, 2008, http://www.christianitytoday.com/ct/2008/may/9.52.html (accessed May 22, 2014).

54. Jim Wallis, "The Bible Is Neither Conservative or Liberal," *God's Politics* (blog), Sojourners, June 12, 2008, http://sojo.net/blogs/2008/06/12/bible-neither-conservative-or-liberal (accessed May 22, 2014).

55. Jim Wallis, *The Great Awakening: Seven Ways to Change the World* (San Francisco: HarperOne, 2009), 195.

56. Billy Hallowell, "Jim Wallis Flip-Flops on Gay Marriage—and Had This to Say About Labeling Same-Sex Opponents 'Bigots,'" TheBlaze, April 9, 2013, http://www.theblaze.com/stories/2013/04/09/jim-wallis-flip-flops-on-gay-marriage-and-had-this-to-say-about-labeling-same-sex-opponents-bigots/ (accessed May 22, 2014).

Chapter 4
Confronting the Same-Sex Dilemma

1. Francis A. Schaeffer and C. Everett Koop, *Whatever Happened to the Human Race?* (Wheaton, IL: Crossway Books, 1983), 2.

2. Aimee Green, "Gender-Neutral Employee Sues for $518,000....," *Oregonian*, February 7, 2014, http://www.oregonlive.com/portland/index.ssf/2014/02/gender-neutral_employee_sues_f.html (accessed May 22, 2014).

3. GLSEN, "Day of Silence," http://glsen.org/participate/programs/day-of-silence (accessed May 22, 2014).

4. Fox News, "School Field Trip to Teacher's Lesbian Wedding Sparks Controversy," October 13, 2008, http://www.foxnews.com/story/2008/10/13/school-field-trip-to-teacher-lesbian-wedding-sparks-controversy/ (accessed May 22, 2014).

5. L. Brent Bozell III, "Degrading 'Degrassi,'" Media Research Center, December 5, 2009, http://www.mrc.org/bozells-column/degrading-degrassi (accessed May 22, 2014); L. Brent Bozell III, "The 'Good News' About Gay Teens," Media Research Center, January 29, 2011, http://www.mrc.org/bozells-column/good-news-about-gay-teens (accessed May 22, 2014).

6. Sally Kohn, "Is Disney Ready for Gay Princess?" CNN.com, January 28, 2014, http://edition.cnn.com/2014/01/28/opinion/kohn-disney-movies/index.html?sr=fb013014gayprincess2p (accessed May 22, 2014).

7. Stoyan Zaimov, "Pastor Andy Stanley Responds to Questions Over Homosexuality Stance," *Christian Post*, May 2, 2012, http://www.christianpost.com/news/pastor-andy-stanley-responds-to-questions-over-homosexuality-stance-74262/ (accessed May 22, 2014); Andy Stanley, "When Gracie Met Truthy (sermon)," http://northpoint.org/messages/christian/part-5 or to watch the entire series, titled Christian, visit http://northpoint.org/messages/christian.

8. John Stott, *Same-Sex Partnerships?* (Grand Rapids, MI: Fleming H. Revell, 1998), 36.

9. Ibid., 43.

10. Joe Dallas and Nancy Heche, *The Complete Christian Guide to Understanding Homosexuality* (Eugene, OR: Harvest House Publishers, 2010), 149.

11. In personal communication with the author.

12. Luke Rosiak, "Fathers Disappear From Households Across America," *Washington Times*, December 25, 2012, http://www.washingtontimes.com/news/2012/dec/25/fathers-disappear-from-households-across-america/?page=all (accessed May 22, 2014).

13. Lydia Saad, "In U.S., 52% Back Law to Legalize Gay Marriage in 50 States," Gallup, July 29, 2013, http://www.gallup.com/poll/163730/back-law-legalize-gay-marriage-states.aspx (accessed May 22, 2014).

14. Maggie Gallagher, "Why Libertarians Should Oppose Same-Sex Marriage," http://www.minnesotaformarriage.com/wp-content/

uploads/2012/01/Why-Libertarians-Should-Oppose-Same-Sex-Marriage
-double-sided-one-page-handout.pdf (accessed May 22, 2014).

15. Peter Sprigg, "Homosexual Parent Study: Summary of Finding,"
Family Research Council, http://www.frc.org/issuebrief/homosexual
-parent-study-summary-of-findings (accessed May 23, 2014); Ana Samuel,
"New Family Structures and the 'No Differences' Claim," Family Struc-
tures Studies, http://www.familystructurestudies.com/summary (accessed
May 23, 2014).

16. Douglas W. Allen, "High School Graduation Rates Among Children of Same-Sex Households," *Review of Economics of the House-
hold* 11, no. 4 (December 2013): 635–658, http://link.springer.com/
article/10.1007%2Fs11150-013-9220-y#page-1 (accessed May 23, 2014).

17. Janice Shaw Crouse, "Five Myths About Same-Sex Marriage,"
Townhall.com, March, 9, 2010, http://townhall.com/columnists/
janiceshawcrouse/2010/03/09/five_myths_about_same_sex_marriage/
page/full (accessed May 23, 2014).

18. Concerned Women for America, "CWA Testifies in Support of
Marriage Before Maryland Senate," February 8, 2011, http://www.cwfa
.org/cwa-testifies-in-support-of-marriage-before-maryland-senate/
(accessed May 23, 2014).

19. Suicide Prevention Resource Center, "Suicide Risk and Prevention
for Lesbian, Gay, Bisexual, and Transgender Youth," 2008, http://www
.sprc.org/sites/sprc.org/files/library/SPRC_LGBT_Youth.pdf (accessed May
23, 2014).

20. Westboro Baptist Church, http://www.godhatesfags.com/ (accessed
May 23, 2014).

21. Imago Dei, http://imagodeicampaign.org/ (accessed May 28, 2014).

22. Elizabeth Dias, "The Imago Dei Campaign: Evangelical Groups Say
Gays Made in God's Image," *Time*, January 20, 2014, http://swampland
.time.com/2014/01/20/the-imago-dei-campaign-evangelical-groups-say
-gays-made-in-gods-image/ (accessed May 23, 2014).

23. Dallas and Heche, *The Complete Christian Guide to Understanding
Homosexuality*, 303.

24. Ibid.

25. In communication with the author.

26. Michael Brown, *Can You Be Gay and Christian?* (Lake Mary, FL:
FrontLine, 2014), 143.

Chapter 5
Unmasking the Social Justice Facade

1. C. S. Lewis, *The Last Battle: The Chronicles of Narnia* (New York:
HarperCollins, 2009).

2. Ryan Messmore, "Seeking Clarity Amidst Confusion About Social Justice," The Foundry, The Heritage Foundation, July 2, 2010, http://blog .heritage.org/2010/07/02/seeking-clarity-amidst-confusion-about-social -justice/ (accessed May 23, 2014).

3. Claiborne, *The Irresistible Revolution*, 153; Shane Claiborne, "Jubilee Party on Wall Street," Two Cents, October 21, 2012, http:// twocents.co/features/jubileeparty2012/ (accessed May 23, 2014).

4. Mark Tooley, "Why Is Tony Campolo Undermining Imprisoned Missionary in North Korea?", *Juicy Ecumenism* (blog), The Institute on Religion & Democracy, March 15, 2014, http://juicyecumenism.com/2014/ 03/15/why-is-tony-campolo-undermining-imprisoned-missionary-in -north-korea/ (accessed May 23, 2014).

5. Shane Claiborne, Facebook post on September 11, 2013, https:// www.facebook.com/ShaneClaiborne/posts/10151547414001371 (accessed May 23, 2014).

6. Mark Tooley, "Shane Claiborne, Chile and the 'First 9-11,'" *Juicy Ecumenism* (blog), The Institute on Religion & Democracy, http:// juicyecumenism.com/2013/09/11/shane-claiborne-chile-and-the-first -9-11/ (accessed May 23, 2014).

7. The Right Scoop, "Jeremiah Wright: Black Liberation Theology Is Socialist," http://therightscoop.com/jeremiah-wright-black-liberation -theology-is-socialist/ (accessed May 23, 2014).

8. J. I. Packer and Thomas C. Oden, *One Faith: The Evangelical Consensus* (Downers Grove, IL: InterVarsity Press, 2004), 149–150.

9. Jeffrey Walton, "Paul Alexander Dismissed from Assemblies of God Clergy," *Juicy Ecumenism* (blog), The Institute on Religion & Democracy, February 10, 2014, http://juicyecumenism.com/2014/02/10/paul -alexander-dismissed-from-assemblies-of-god-clergy/ (accessed May 23, 2014).

10. Ibid., emphasis added.

11. Carol Keehan, "What's Right About Obamacare?" *Sojourners*, March 2014, http://sojo.net/magazine/2014/01-0/whats-right-about -obamacare (accessed May 23, 2014).

12. Ibid.

13. Benjamin L. Corey, "10 Things You Can't Do and Still Call Yourself 'Pro-Life,'" *Formerly Fundie* (blog), Patheos, June 21, 2013, http://www .patheos.com/blogs/formerlyfundie/pro-life-or-pro-birth/ (accessed May 23, 2014).

14. John Blake, "Evangelical Leader Takes on Beck for Assailing Social Justice Churches," CNN, March 12, 2010, http://www.cnn.com/2010/ LIVING/03/12/beck.boycott/ (accessed May 23, 2014).

15. Beverly LaHaye, *The Desires of a Woman's Heart* (Wheaton, IL: Tyndale House, 1995), 205.

16. John Stossel and Kristina Kendall, "Who Gives and Who Doesn't," ABC News, November 28, 2006, http://abcnews.go.com/2020/story?id=2682730&page=1 (accessed May 23, 2014).

17. Texas Christian University, "Church Ties," http://www.tcu.edu/96.asp (accessed May 23, 2014).

18. John Andrew Willis, "How Christian Is Texas Christian University," *Horned Frog Blog*, TCU Admission Office, January 14, 2013, http://tcuadmission.wordpress.com/2013/01/14/how-christian-is-texas-christian-university/ (accessed May 23, 2014).

19. Concerned Women for America, "Christians on Diversity in the Academy," http://www.cwfa.org/wp-content/uploads/2014/03/AzuzaConfDocs_032410.pdf (accessed May 23, 2014).

20. Ibid., 13.

21. Ibid., 18, emphasis added.

22. In communication with the author, March 7, 2013.

23. *First Things*, "College Rankings," November 2010, http://www.firstthings.com/article/2010/11/college-rankings (accessed May 23, 2014).

24. Chelsen Vicari, "Future of Christianity Depends on LGBTQ, Minorities, and Global Church, say C21 Speakers," *Juicy Ecumenism* (blog), The Institute on Religion & Democracy, January 13, 2014, http://juicyecumenism.com/2014/01/13/the-future-of-christianity-depends-on-the-lgbtq-minorities-poor-and-global-communities-says-c21-speakers/ (accessed June 20, 2014).

25. Ibid.

Chapter 6
Unveiling the Jesus Feminists

1. Elisabeth Elliot, *Let Me Be a Woman* (Carol Stream, IL: Tyndale House, 1976), 43.

2. Taylor Antrim, "Superman Returns: Tim Tebow Touches Down in New York," *Vogue*, http://www.vogue.com/magazine/article/superman-returns-tim-tebow/#1 (accessed May 23, 2014).

3. Jenna Sauers, "Tim Tebow Tells *Vogue* His Perfect Woman Is Hot, Kind, and Servile," *Jezebel* (blog), http://jezebel.com/5945247/tim-tebows-perfect-woman-is-hot-kind-and-servile (accessed May 23, 2014).

4. Russell D. Moore, "Is Tim Tebow a Chauvinist," *Moore to the Point* (blog), http://www.russellmoore.com/2012/09/22/is-tim-tebow-a-chauvinist/ (accessed May 23, 2014).

5. CNN, "Bachmann Explains 'Submissive' Marriage," http://cnn.com/video/?/video/bestoftv/2011/08/12/exp.nr.bachmann.submission.cnn (accessed May 23, 2014).

6. YouTube.com, "Submission Impossible: Michele Bachmann Reiterates Her 'Submissiveness' to her Husband," http://www.youtube.com/watch?v=15KPx6ezo6c (accessed May 23, 2014).

7. Ibid.

8. Phyllis Schlafly and Suzanne Venker, *The Flipside of Feminism* (New York: WND Books, 2011), 16.

9. Chelsen Vicari, "Seminary Revives the Art of Homemaking," *Juicy Ecumenism* (blog), The Institute on Religion & Democracy, November 5, 2013, http://juicyecumenism.com/2013/11/05/seminary-revives-the-art-of-homemaking/ (accessed May 23, 2014).

10. Alissa Quart, "'I Am a Feminist Because Jesus Made Me One,'" *New York Magazine*, http://nymag.com/thecut/2013/01/jesus-feminists.html (accessed May 23, 2014).

11. Sarah Bessey, *Jesus Feminist* (New York: Howard Books, 2013), 13–14.

12. Ibid.

13. Ibid., 15.

14. Ibid., 11.

15. Ibid., 12.

16. Laura Turner, "The Christian F-Word," *Christianity Today*, September 25, 2013, http://www.christianitytoday.com/women/2013/september/christian-f-word.html?paging=off (accessed May 24, 2014).

17. Ibid.

18. Candi Finch, "Before You Swallow the Pill," Biblical Woman, January 17, 2012, http://www.biblicalwoman.com/2012/01/17/before-you-swallow-the-pill/ (accessed June 5, 2014).

19. Ravi Zacharias's Facebook page, accessed May 28, 2014 https://www.facebook.com/ravizacharias/posts/10151820628361813.

20. Crumpton, "The Worst Lie of Election 2012: Women Are 'Shiny Objects' of 'Distraction,'" emphasis added.

21. Ibid.

22. Evans, "Privilege and the Pill."

23. Mary Kassian, *The Feminine Gospel: The Movement to Unite Feminism Within the Church* (Wheaton, IL: Crossway Books, 1992), 18.

24. Simone de Beauvoir, *The Second Sex* (New York: Random House Inc., 1989), 724.

25. Marianne Schnall, "Q&A," GloriaSteinem.com, http://www.gloriasteinem.com/qa/ (accessed May 24, 2014).

26. Susan B. Anthony List, "Early Suffragists," http://www.sba-list.org/movement/notable-women/early-suffragists (accessed May 24, 2014).

27. Ibid.

28. Mary Eberstadt, *Adam and Eve After the Pill* (San Francisco: Ignatius Press, 2012), 32.

29. ABC News, "Porn Profits: Corporate America's Secret," http://abcnews.go.com/Primetime/story?id=132001 (accessed May 24, 2014).

30. 10news.com, "Thousands of Woman Reporting Severe Medical Reactions to Essure Birth Control," October 3, 2013, http://www.10news.com/news/investigations/thousands-of-women-reporting-severe-medical-reactions-to-essure-birth-control-100313 (accessed May 24, 2014).

31. National Cancer Institute, "Oral Contraceptives and Cancer Risk," http://www.cancer.gov/cancertopics/factsheet/Risk/oral-contraceptives (accessed May 24, 2014).

32. WebMD.com, "YAZ 28 Oral," http://tinyurl.com/yaz28oral (accessed May 23, 2014).

33. Jessica Valenti, *Full Frontal Feminism: A Young Woman's Guide to Why Feminism Matters* (Emeryville, CA: Seal Press, 2007), 151.

34. In communication with the author.

35. Keller, "Rachel Held Evans."

36. Ibid.

37. Emanuella Grinberg, "Helen Gurley Brown's Complicated Feminist Legacy," CNN, August 19, 2012, http://www.cnn.com/2012/08/17/living/helen-gurley-brown-legacy/ (accessed May 24, 2014).

38. Liz Jones, "She Was the Legendary Cosmo Editor Who...Sold Us an Impossible Dream," Mail Online, August 14, 2012, http://www.dailymail.co.uk/femail/article-2188494/Helen-Gurley-Brown-genius-says-Liz-Jones-sold-impossible-dream.html (accessed May 24, 2014).

39. Rebecca Walker, "How My Mother's Fanatical Views Tore Us Apart," Mail Online, May 23, 2008, http://www.dailymail.co.uk/femail/article-1021293/How-mothers-fanatical-feminist-views-tore-apart-daughter-The-Color-Purple-author.html (accessed May 23, 2014).

40. Ibid.

41. Dale O'Leary, "The Oppressed Lives of Stay-at-Homes Moms," *Crisis Magazine*, April 27, 2012, http://www.crisismagazine.com/2012/the-oppressed-lives-of-stay-at-home-moms (accessed May 24, 2014).

42. Dorothy Patterson, "The Universal Spare Part," Southwestern Baptist Theological Seminary, October 26, 2013, http://www.swbts.edu/index.cfm/resources/?action=public:library.default&collection=123 (accessed May 24, 2014).

43. *Telegraph*, "Traditional Acts of Chivalry Frowned Upon as 'Suspicious,'" http://www.telegraph.co.uk/news/newstopics/howaboutthat/9800488/Traditional-acts-of-chivalry-frowned-upon-as-suspicious.html (accessed May 23, 2014).

44. Sheryl Sandberg, *Lean In: Women, Work, and the Will to Lead* (New York: Random House, 2013), 14.

45. Jonathan Merritt, "Was Jesus a Feminist? Author Sarah Bessey Thinks So," Religion News Service, http://jonathanmerritt.religionnews

.com/2013/11/11/feminism-sarah-bessey-thinks-so/ (accessed May 23, 2014).

46. Beverly LaHaye, *Who But a Woman?* (Nashville: Thomas Nelson Publishers, 1984), 31.

47. Ibid.

48. Concerned Women for America, "Judge Voids North Dakota 'Heartbeat' Abortion Law," April 17, 2014, http://www.cwfa.org/judge -voids-north-dakota-heartbeat-abortion-law/ (accessed May 24, 2014). See conclusion of press release.

Chapter 7
Defending Every Life

1. Ronald Reagan, "Reagan-Anderson Presidential Debate in Baltimore," September 21, 1980 http://www.presidency.ucsb.edu/ws/index .php?pid=29407 (accessed May 24, 2014).

2. Dr. Seuss, *Horton Hears a Who!* (New York: Random House, 1982).

3. Steve Ertelt, "55,772,015 Abortions in America Since Roe vs. Wade in 1973," LifeNews.com, January 18, 2013, http://www.lifenews.com/ 2013/01/18/55772015-abortions-in-america-since-roe-vs-wade-in-1973/ (accessed May 24, 2014).

4. National Right to Life Committee, "National Right to Life Mourns the Death of Former Congressman Henry J. Hyde," November 29, 2007, http://www.nrlc.org/archive/press_releases_new/Mourns%20Henry%20 Hyde.htm (accessed May 24, 2014).

5. American Life League, "Abortion," http://www.all.org/nav/index/ heading/OQ/cat/MzQ/id/NjA3OQ/ (accessed May 24, 2014).

6. Marcia Pally, "The Politics of the 'New Evangelicals': Rethinking Abortion and Gay Marriage," ABC Religion and Ethics, February 9, 2013, http://www.abc.net.au/religion/articles/2013/02/09/3686782.htm (accessed May 24, 2014).

7. Dave Andrusko, "Pro-Life Perspectives: 'Black Pro-Life Pioneers— Mildred Jefferson,'" National Right to Life News, February 3, 2013, http:// www.nationalrighttolifenews.org/news/2012/02/pro-life-perspectives -black-pro-life-pioneers-mildred-jefferson/#.Uw5abc427h0 (accessed May 23, 2014).

8. Lydia Saad, "U.S. Still Split on Abortion: 47% Pro-Choice, 46% Pro-Life," Gallup, May 22, 2014, http://www.gallup.com/poll/170249/ split-abortion-pro-choice-pro-life.aspx?utm_source=alert&utm_medium =email&utm_campaign=syndication&utm_content=morelink&utm_ term=Politics (accessed May 24, 2014)

9. Ibid.

10. Juliet Eilperin, "Antiabortion Measures Gain Momentum in States," *Washington Post*, April 11, 2013, http://www.washingtonpost.com/

politics/antiabortion-measures-gain-momentum-in-the-states/2013/04/11/
686b9492-a2d3-11e2-9c03-6952ff305f35_story.html (accessed May 24,
2014).

11. Chris McComb, "Teens Lean Conservative on Abortion," Gallup,
November 18, 2003, http://www.gallup.com/poll/9715/teens-lean
-conservative-abortion.aspx (accessed May 28, 2014).

12. Saad, "U.S. Still Split on Abortion: 47% Pro-Choice, 46% Pro-Life."

13. Fox News, "Planned Parenthood Receives Record Amount of Tax-
payer Support," January 8, 2013, http://www.foxnews.com/politics/2013/
01/08/planned-parenthood-receives-record-amount-taxpayer-support/
(accessed May 23, 2014).

14. Mallory Quigley, "Planned Parenthood Report: $540 Million in
Tax Dollars, 327,000 Abortions," LifeNews.com, http://www.lifenews
.com/2013/12/11/planned-parenthood-report-540-million-in-tax-dollars
-327000-abortions/ (accessed May 24, 2014); Planned Parenthood Annual
Report 2012–2013, http://issuu.com/actionfund/docs/ar-fy13_111213_vf_
rev3_issuu/15?e=1994783/5940818 (accessed May 23, 2014).

15. Susan B. Anthony List, "Fact Sheet: Planned Parenthood's 2012-
2013 Annual Report," http://www.sba-list.org/sites/default/files/content/
shared/pp_fact_sheet_2012_2013_annual_report.pdf (accessed May 23,
2014).

16. George Grant, *Grand Illusions: The Legacy of Planned Parenthood*
(Franklin, TN: Adroit Press, 1988), 27.

17. Susan W. Enouen, "New Research Shows Planned Parenthood
Targets Minority Neighborhoods," *Life Issues Connector*, October 2012,
http://www.protectingblacklife.org/pdf/PP-Targets-10-2012.pdf (accessed
May 24, 2014).

18. Michael W. Chapman, "NYC: More Black Babies Killed by Abortion Than Born," cnsnews.com, February 20, 2014, http://www.cnsnews
.com/news/article/michael-w-chapman/nyc-more-black-babies-killed
-abortion-born (accessed May 24, 2014).

19. Alveda King, "How Can Blacks Survive if We Murder Our Children?", LifeNews.com, February 18, 2013, http://www.lifenews.com/2013/
02/18/alveda-king-how-can-blacks-survive-if-we-murder-our-children/
(accessed May 24, 2014).

20. Josiah Ryan, "Planned Parenthood Agreed to Accept Race-
Motivated Donations," cnsnews.com, July 7, 2008, http://cnsnews.com/
node/7753 (accessed May 24, 2014).

21. To read their comments, see Jonathan Merritt, "3 Reasons the
Abortion Rate Is Lowest Since Roe v. Wade," Religion News Service, February 19, 2014, http://jonathanmerritt.religionnews.com/2014/02/19/3
-reasons-abortion-rate-plummeted/ (accessed May 24, 2014); Evans,
"Privilege and the Pill." Religion News Services, "Family Planning Vital

to Child Survival Say Christian Health Experts at Capitol Hill Event," December 4, 2013, http://pressreleases.religionnews.com/2013/12/04/ family-planning-vital-child-survival-say-christian-health-experts-capitol -hill-event/ (accessed May 24, 2014).

22. Rachel K. Jones, Jacqueline E. Darroch, and Stanley K. Henshaw, "Contraceptive Use Among U.S. Women Having Abortions in 2000–2001," Guttmacher Institute, http://www.guttmacher.org/pubs/journals/3429402 .pdf (accessed May 24, 2014); Ross Douthat, "The 'Safe, Legal, Rare' Illusion," *New York Times*, February 18, 2012, http://www.nytimes.com/ 2012/02/19/opinion/sunday/douthat-the-safe-legal-rare-illusion.html (accessed May 24, 2014).

23. Centers for Disease Control and Prevention, "Prepregnancy Contraceptive Use Among Teens....," January 20, 2014, http://www.cdc.gov/ mmwr/preview/mmwrhtml/mm6102a1.htm?s_cid=mm6102a1_e (accessed May 24, 2014).

24. José Luis Dueñas, Iñaki Lete, Rafael Bermejo, et al., "Trends in the Use of Contraceptive Methods and Voluntary Interruption of Pregnancy in the Spanish Population....," *Contraception* 83, no. 1 (January 2011): 82–87, http://www.ncbi.nlm.nih.gov/pubmed/21134508 (accessed June 25, 2014).

25. Planned Parenthood, "In-Clinic Abortion Procedures," http://www .plannedparenthood.org/health-topics/abortion/in-clinic-abortion -procedures-4359.asp (accessed May 24, 2014).

26. Reproductive Health Access Project, "Pharmacies With Low-Cost Birth Control Pills," http://www.reproductiveaccess.org/contraception/ lowcost_pills.htm (accessed May 24, 2014).

27. *USA Today*, "Authorities: Woman Died From Abortion Complications," June 12, 2013, http://www.usatoday.com/story/news/nation/2013/ 02/21/woman-late-term-abortion-death/1935799/ (accessed May 24, 2014).

28. Operation Rescue, "Death Certificate Confirms Abortion, not Fetal Anomaly, Responsible for Woman's Death," March 13, 2013, http://www .operationrescue.org/archives/death-certificate-confirms-abortion-not -fetal-anomaly-responsible-for-womans-death/ (accessed May 24, 2014).

29. Elizabeth Shadigian, "Reviewing the Evidence, Breaking the Silence: Long-Term Physical and Psychological health Consequences of Induced Abortion," in Erika Bachiochi, ed., *The Cost of "Choice"* (San Francisco: Encounter Books, 2004), 64.

30. David Reardon, *Aborted Women: Silent No More* (Chicago: Loyola University Press, 1987), 119–129.

31. David Bailey, "Appeals Court Upholds South Dakota Abortion Law's Suicide Advisory," Reuters, July 24, 2012, http://www.reuters.com/ article/2012/07/24/us-usa-abortion-southdakota-idUSBRE86N1DM 20120724 (accessed May 24, 2014).

32. Concerned Women for America, "Casualty of Abortion," February 19, 2013, http://www.cwfa.org/casualty-of-abortion/ (accessed May 24, 2014).

33. Ibid.

34. Pam Belluck, "Pregnancy Centers Gain Influence in Anti-Abortion Arena," *New York Times,* January 4, 2013, http://www.nytimes.com/2013/ 01/05/health/pregnancy-centers-gain-influence-in-anti-abortion-fight .html?pagewanted=all&_r=0 (accessed May 24, 2014).

35. Lauren Enriquez, "Abortions Statistics: 1.2 Million Babies Die Every Year From Abortions," LifeNews.com, July 1, 2013, http://www .lifenews.com/2013/07/01/abortion-statistics-1-2-million-babies-die-every -year-from-abortions/ (accessed May 24, 2014).

36. Lawrence B. Finer, Lori F. Frohwirth, Lindsay A. Dauphinee, Susheela Singh, and Ann M. Moore, "Reasons U.S. Women Have Abortions: Quantitative and Qualitative Perspectives," Guttmacher Institute, https:// www.guttmacher.org/pubs/journals/3711005.pdf (accessed May 23, 2014).

37. Ibid.

38. John Ensor and Scott Klusendorf, *Stand for Life: A Student's Guide for Making the Case and Saving Lives* (Peabody, MA: Hendrickson Publishers Marketing, 2012), 65.

39. The Radiance Foundation, "Ryan Scott Bomberger," http://www .theradiancefoundation.org/ryan/ (accessed May 24, 2014).

40. Marvin Olasky, "Radiating Truth," *World,* January 25, 2014, http:// www.worldmag.com/2014/01/radiating_truth/page2 (accessed May 24, 2014).

41. Amy Harmon, "Prenatal Test Puts Down Syndrome in Hard Focus," *New York Times,* May 9, 2007, http://www.nytimes.com/2007/05/09/us/ 09down.html?_r=0 (accessed May 24, 2014).

42. Concerned Women for America, "World Down Syndrome Day," http://www.cwfa.org/world-down-syndrome-day-2/ (accessed May 24, 2014).

43. Tim Harris, "Breakfast, Lunch and Hugs at Tim's Place," CNN, July 10, 2013, http://www.cnn.com/2013/07/10/health/human-factor -harris/ (accessed May 24, 2014).

44. Abby Ellin, "Man With Down Syndrome Runs N.M. Restaurant," ABC News, March 4, 2013, http://abcnews.go.com/blogs/business/2013/ 03/man-with-down-syndrome-runs-n-m-restaurant/ (accessed May 24, 2014).

45. Concerned Women for America, "Facts About Down Syndrome," http://www.cwfa.org/downsyndromebrochure/facts.shtml (accessed May 24, 2014).

46. Mark Leach, "One of the Most Compassionate Missions in the United States," Down Syndrome Prenatal Testing, April 17, 2013, http://

www.downsyndromeprenataltesting.com/one-of-the-most-compassionate
-missions-in-the-united-states/ (accessed May 24, 2014).

47. Lauren Enriquez, "Adopted Paralympic Athlete Loves Birth Mother 'Because She Gave Me Life'," Live Action News, http://liveactionnews.org/ adopted-paralympic-athlete-loves-birth-mother-because-she-gave-me -life/ (accessed May 24, 2014).

48. Chelsea Patterson, "Adoption: The Period to the Pro-Life Sentence," The Ethics & Religious Liberty Commission, January 22, 2014, http://erlc .com/article/adoption-the-period-to-the-pro-life-sentence (accessed May 24, 2014).

49. *USA Today*, "Belgian Senate OKs Child Euthanasia Bill," December 12, 2013, http://www.usatoday.com/story/news/world/2013/12/12/belgium -senate-child-euthanasia/4000713/ (accessed May 24, 2014).

50. Celeste McGovern, "Children and Euthanasia: Belgium Votes to Remove Age Limits on 'Mercy Killing,'" *National Catholic Register*, February 18, 2014, http://www.ncregister.com/daily-news/children-and -euthanasia-belgium-votes-to-remove-all-age-limits-on-mercy-kil (accessed May 23, 2014).

51. Steven Ertelt, "MSNBC Host: Life Begins When Parents Say It Does, Not Based on Science," LifeNews.com, http://www.lifenews.com/ 2013/07/23/msnbc-host-life-begins-when-parents-say-it-does-not-based -on-science/ (accessed May 23, 2014).

52. Robert P. George, "Bernard Nathanson: A Life Transformed by Truth," Public Discourse, The Witherspoon Institute, February 27, 2011, http://www.thepublicdiscourse.com/2011/02/2806/ (accessed May 23, 2014).

Chapter 8
Opposing Christian Persecution

1. Thomas Jefferson, in a letter to Philip Mazzei, The Jefferson Monticello, http://www.monticello.org/site/research-and-collections/philip -mazzei (accessed June 25, 2014).

2. Tom Ehrich, "Get Real About 'Religious Freedom,'" Morning Walk Media, February 26, 2014, http://www.morningwalkmedia.com/tom -ehrich-on-life-faith/2014/2/26/get-real-about-religious-freedom (accessed May 23, 2014); Tom Ehrich, "Commentary: A Parched Patch of Prejudice," Religion News Service, March 4, 2014, http://www.religionnews.com/ 2014/03/04/commentary-parched-patch-prejudice/ (accessed May 24, 2014).

3. Napp Nazworth, "Critics of Arizona Bill Are 'Trying to Deceive You,' Liberal and Conservative Law Professors Tell Gov. Brewer," *Christian Post*, http://www.christianpost.com/news/critics-of-arizona-bill-are

-trying-to-deceive-you-liberal-and-conservative-law-professors-tell-gov
-brewer-115273/ (accessed May 24, 2014).

4. Kirsten Powers, "Jim Crow Laws for Gays and Lesbians?",
USA Today, February 19, 2014, http://www.usatoday.com/story/
opinion/2014/02/18/gays-lesbians-kansas-bill-religious-freedom
-christians-column/5588643/ (accessed May 24, 2014).

5. Ibid.

6. Mario Diaz, "Stanley & Powers Miss the Mark in Comparing Jim
Crow Laws to Gay Marriage," *Christian Post*, February 21, 2014, http://
www.christianpost.com/news/kirsten-powers-misses-the-mark-in
-comparing-jim-crow-laws-to-gay-marriage-115013/ (accessed May 24,
2014).

7. Joe Carter, "Since Jesus Ate With Sinners, Do I Have to Eat at the
Strip Club's Buffet?", The Gospel Coalition, February 26, 2014, http://
thegospelcoalition.org/blogs/tgc/2014/02/26/since-jesus-ate-with-sinners
-do-i-have-to-eat-at-the-strip-clubs-buffet/ (accessed May 24, 2014).

8. Powers, "Jim Crow Laws for Gays and Lesbians?"

9. McKay Coppins, "A New Mission for the Religious Right?",
BuzzFeed Politics, February 27, 2014, http://www.buzzfeed.com/
mckaycoppins/a-new-mission-for-the-religious-right (accessed May 24,
2014).

10. The Federalist Papers, "James Madison Quotes," http://www
.thefederalistpapers.org/founders/james-madison-quotes (accessed May 23,
2014).

11. James Joyner, "Air Force Academy Commandant John Weida
Under Review," *Outside the Beltway* (blog), June 9, 2005, http://www
.outsidethebeltway.com/ap_air_force_academy_chief_under_review_-_
yahoo_news/ (accessed May 24, 2014).

12. Todd Starnes, "Army Labeled Evangelicals as Religious Extremists,"
Fox News, http://radio.foxnews.com/toddstarnes/top-stories/army-labeled
-evangelicals-as-religious-extremism.html (accessed May 24, 2014).

13. Gordon James Klingenschmitt, "Five Chaplains Lose Jobs for
Praying 'In Jesus' Name'....," Christian News Wire, http://www
.christiannewswire.com/news/275958004.html (accessed May 24, 2014);
YouTube.com, "700 Club (After Rally) Virginia Police Chaplains Forced
Out for Praying 'in Jesus Name,'" https://www.youtube.com/watch?v=0_
QoDHlsodw (accessed May 24, 2014).

14. Huffington Post, "Joe Moreno, Chicago Alderman, Plans to Block
Planned Chick-fil-A Restaurant in Logan Square," July 25, 2012, http://
www.huffingtonpost.com/2012/07/25/joe-moreno-chicago-alderm_n_
1701646.html (accessed May 23, 2014).

15. Megyn Kelly, "Two Schools Cancel Christmas Toy Drive After
Lawsuit Threat," Fox News, November 21, 2013, http://video.foxnews

.com/v/2857704491001/two-schools-cancel-christmas-toy-drive-after
-lawsuit-threat/#sp=show-clips (accessed May 24, 2014).

16. Nelson Garcia, "SkyView Academy Parents Continue Toy Drive
Despite Lawsuit Threat to School," 9News.com, November 20, 2013,
http://archive.9news.com/news/story.aspx?storyid=365452 (accessed May
24, 2014).

17. Matthew Clark, "What Is Your Religious Liberty Worth to You?",
ACLJ, November 12, 2013, http://aclj.org/obamacare/what-is-your
-religious-liberty-worth-to-you (accessed May 24, 2014).

18. Stand-Up Comedy Portal, "Jon Stewart," http://standupcomedy
portal.com/quotes/7660 (accessed May 24, 2014).

19. Candida Moss, "The Myth of Christian Persecution," Huffington
Post, http://www.huffingtonpost.com/candida-moss/the-myth-of
-christian-persecution_b_2901880.html (accessed May 24, 2014).

20. Tim Johnston, "Three Indonesian Girls Beaded," BBC News,
October 29, 2005, http://news.bbc.co.uk/2/hi/asia-pacific/4387604.stm
(accessed May 24, 2014).

21. Reuters, "Seven Egyptian Christians Found Shot Execution-
Style on Libyan Beach," February 24, 2014, http://www.reuters.com/
article/2014/02/24/us-libya-egyptians-idUSBREA1N13V20140224
(accessed May 24, 2014).

22. Jack Healy, "Exodus From North Signals Iraqi Christians' Slow
Decline," March 10, 2012, http://www.nytimes.com/2012/03/11/world/
middleeast/exodus-from-north-signals-iraqi-christians-decline.html
?pagewanted=all&_r=0 (accessed May 24, 2014).

23. *New York Post*, "The Forgotten Arab Christians," March 2, 2014,
http://nypost.com/2014/03/02/the-forgotten-arab-christians/ (accessed
May 24, 2014).

24. *New York Post*, "Sentenced to Death for a Sip of Water," August 25,
2013, http://nypost.com/2013/08/25/sentenced-to-death-for-a-sip-of-water/
(accessed May 23, 2014).

25. Jordan Sekulow, "A Glimmer of Hope for American Pastor
Saeed….," January 27, 2014, http://aclj.org/iran/a-glimmer-of-hope
-american-pastor-saeed-as-iran-foreign-minister-suggests-clemency
-possible (accessed May 24, 2014); Todd Starnes, *God Less America* (Lake
Mary, FL: FrontLine, 2014), 43–48.

26. Armando Valladares, *Against All Hope* (San Francisco: Encounter
Books, 2001), 35.

27. Armando Valladares, "So Persecuted They the Prophets," *Christianity and Democracy*, August/Sept. 1983, 3–4; Armando Valladares,
"Remarks and Poems," *Crisis Magazine*, September 1, 1983, http://www
.crisismagazine.com/1983/remarks-and-poems (accessed May 24, 2014).

28. Jonathan Merritt, "In the Middle East, Not America, Christians Are Actually Persecuted," Religion News Service, April 3, 2013, http://jonathanmerritt.religionnews.com/2013/04/03/in-the-middle-east-not-america-christians-are-actually-persecuted/ (accessed May 24, 2014).

29. Ibid.

30. Brian McLaren, "Muslims, Christians, Jews, and Peace (Part 1)," *Brian D. McLaren* (blog), http://brianmclaren.net/archives/blog/muslims-christians-and-violence.html (accessed May 24, 2014).

31. Faith McDonnell, "Brian McLaren's Five Errors about Christian Persecution, Part One," *Juicy Ecumenism* (blog), The Institute on Religion & Democracy, October 10, 2013, http://juicyecumenism.com/2013/10/10/an-old-kind-of-christianity-5-things-brian-mclaren-got-wrong-about-the-persecuted-church/ (accessed May 24, 2014).

32. Ibid.

33. Robert Spencer, "New Moderate Iran Executes Two Gay Men and Hands Down Death Sentence for 'Insulting the Prophet,'" Jihad Watch, March 3, 2014, http://www.jihadwatch.org/2014/03/new-moderate-iran-executes-two-gay-men-and-hands-down-death-sentence-for-insulting-the-prophet (accessed May 24, 2014).

34. Eric Metaxas, *Amazing Grace* (San Francisco: HarperCollins Publishers, 2007), 69–71.

35. Ibid., 144.

Chapter 9
Supporting Israel

1. Dan Gilgoff, "John Hagee Interviews Elie Wiesel," *US News & World Report*, September 3, 2009, http://www.usnews.com/news/blogs/god-and-country/2009/09/03/john-hagee-interviews-elie-wiesel (accessed May 27, 2014).

2. Quoted in David Brog, *Standing With Israel* (Lake Mary, FL: FrontLine, 2006), 235.

3. Ibid., 236.

4. John Hagee, *Jerusalem Countdown* (Lake Mary, FL: FrontLine, 2006), 196–200.

5. Ibid., 196.

6. Anti-Defamation League, "U.S. Presidents and the State of Israel," http://www.adl.org/israel-international/israel-middle-east/content/us-presidents-and-Israel.html (accessed May 27, 2014).

7. Michael Lipka, "More White Evangelicals Than American Jews Say God Gave Israel to the Jewish People," *Pew Research Center*, October 3, 2013, http://www.pewresearch.org/fact-tank/2013/10/03/more-white-evangelicals-than-american-jews-say-god-gave-israel-to-the-jewish-people/ (accessed May 27, 2014).

8. Tricia Aven, "Telos Group Promotes Anti-Zionist Narrative in Evangelical Community," *Camera*, March 18, 2014, http://www.camera .org/index.asp?x_context=2&x_outlet=118&x_article=2672 (accessed May 27, 2014).

9. Hybels, "The Israeli-Palestinian Conflict: Six Things I Believe."

10. Ibid.

11. Mark Tooley, "Lynne Hybels, Evangelicals, and Israel," *First Things*, December 30, 2013, http://www.firstthings.com/web-exclusives/2013/12/ lynne-hybels-evangelicals-and-israel (accessed May 27, 2014).

12. Luke Moon, in communication with the author.

13. Vimeo.com, "CATC 2014: 'Dialogue on Replacement Theology': Gary Burge & Daniel Juster," http://vimeo.com/89570014 (accessed May 27, 2014).

14. Daniel Greenfield, "Outraged Protest Tours—The Tourism Package for Leftists Who Hate Israel," Canada Free Press, July 20, 2011, http:// www.canadafreepress.com/index.php/article/38643 (accessed May 23, 2014).

15. Vimeo.com, "CATC 2014: 'Dialogue on Replacement Theology': Gary Burge & Daniel Juster."

16. Ibid.

17. Spiegel Online International, "SPIEGEL Interview With Steven Spielberg: 'I Would Die for Israel,'" January 26, 2006, http://www.spiegel .de/international/spiegel/spiegel-interview-with-steven-spielberg-i-would -die-for-israel-a-397378.html (accessed May 27, 2014).

18. CBS News, "The Father of Modern Terrorism," November 12, 2004, http://www.cbsnews.com/news/the-father-of-modern-terrorism/ (accessed May 27, 2014).

19. Lela Gilbert, *Saturday People, Sunday People* (New York: Encounter Books, 2012), 156.

20. Ibid., 159

21. *Jspace News*, "Golda Meir: Israel's First Female Prime Minister," December 6, 2013, http://www.jspacenews.com/golda-meir-israel-first -female-prime-minister/ (accessed May 13, 2014).

22. *Jewish Press*, "California Students Testify About Anti-Semitism on Campus," March 27, 2014, http://www.jewishpress.com/indepth/ california-students-testify-about-anti-semitism-on-campus/2014/03/27/ (accessed May 27, 2014).

23. Ibid.

24. Ibid.

25. Ibid.

26. UN Watch, "Anti-Israel Resolutions at the HRC," http://www .unwatch.org/site/c.bdKKISNqEmG/b.3820041/ (accessed May 27, 2014).

27. United Nations, "Secretary-General Urges Human Rights Activists to 'Fill Leadership Vacuum', Hold World Leaders to Account….," http://www.un.org/News/Press/docs/2006/sgsm10788.doc.htm (accessed May 27, 2014).

28. UN Watch, "Anti-Israel Resolutions at the HRC."

29. Institute for Middle East Understanding, "Are All Palestinians Muslim?" http://imeu.net/news/article0042.shtml (accessed May 27, 2014).

30. YouTube.com, "Christy a Palestinian Christian's Plea to Dr. Saeb Erekat," https://www.youtube.com/watch?v=YzCAqXrBGtU (accessed May 27, 2014).

31. Ibid.

32. Ibid.

33. Ibid.

34. Ibid.

35. Hagee, *Jerusalem Countdown*, 33.

36. Robert Nicholson, "Who's Afraid of Christian Zionism?", *Times of Israel*, February 27, 2014, http://blogs.timesofisrael.com/zionists-who-love-jesus/ (accessed May 27, 2014).

37. Ibid.

38. Ibid

39. Ibid

40. Ibid.

Chapter 10
Speaking Truth in Love

1. Martin Luther King Jr., "Nobel Prize Acceptance Speech," December 10, 1964, http://www.nobelprize.org/nobel_prizes/peace/laureates/1964/king-acceptance_en.html?print=1#.U1XE-_ldWww (accessed May 27, 2014).

2. YouTube.com, "Ravi Zacharias—No Reserves, No Retreats, No Regrets," https://www.youtube.com/watch?v=2BtzifEveNQ (accessed May 27, 2014).

3. John Piper, "Truth and Love," Desiring God, May 15, 2000, http://www.desiringgod.org/articles/truth-and-love (accessed May 27, 2014).

4. NPR.org, "West Side Story: The Murder That Shocked New York," July 30, 2007, http://www.npr.org/templates/story/story.php?storyId=12350113 (accessed May 27, 2014).

5. David Wilkerson, "How It All Began," World Challenge, http://www.worldchallenge.org/page.aspx?pid=451 (accessed May 23, 2014).

6. Ibid.

7. *The Cross and the Switchblade*, directed by Don Murray (N.p.: Ross Records, 2003), DVD; Imdb.com, "*The Cross and the Switchblade* Quotes," http://www.imdb.com/title/tt0068428/quotes (accessed May 27, 2014).

8. Tony Reinke, "Speaking the Truth in Love," Desiring God, August 19, 2012, http://www.desiringgod.org/blog/posts/speaking-the-truth-in -love (accessed May 27, 2014).

9. Bruce Frohnen, "The Cult of Niceness," The Imaginative Conservative, http://www.theimaginativeconservative.org/2013/11/cult-niceness .html (accessed May 27, 2014).

10. Billy Graham, *Revival in Our Time* (Wheaton, IL: Van Kampen Press, 1950).

11. Billy Graham, "The Cross," Billy Graham Evangelistic Association, http://myhopewithbillygraham.org/programs/the-cross/ (accessed May 27, 2014).

12. Rob Bell, "What We Talk About When We Talk About God," interview with Jane Shaw, Grace Cathedral, March 17, 2013, http://www .gracecathedral.org/cathedral-life/worship/listen/detail.php?fid=182 (accessed May 27, 2014).

13. Sanneh, "The Hell-Raiser."

14. *Christianity Today*, "Jonathan Edwards: Americas Greatest Theologian," August 8, 2008, http://www.christianitytoday.com/ch/ 131christians/theologians/edwards.html (accessed May 27, 2014).

15. Jonathan Edwards, "Sinners in the Hands of an Angry God," http:// digitalcommons.unl.edu/cgi/viewcontent.cgi?article=1053&context=etas (accessed May 27, 2014).

16. Paul Strand, "Brazil: The Fire of Revival," CBN News, http://www .cbn.com/tv/1420562208001 (accessed May 27, 2014).

Chapter 11
Living Out Bold Faith

1. *New York Times*, "John Calvin Coolidge, 30th President," http:// events.nytimes.com/learning/general/specials/elections/1924/coolidge .html (accessed June 25, 2014).

2. Julian Simon, "More People, Greater Wealth, More Resources, Healthier Environment," http://www.juliansimon.com/writings/Articles/ POPENVI2.txt (accessed May 28, 2014).

3. Joshua Harris, *Humble Orthodoxy: Holding the Truth High Without Putting People Down* (Colorado Springs: Multnomah Books, 2013).

4. James Arne Nestingen, *Martin Luther: A Life* (Minneapolis: Fortress Press, 2003), 46.

5. Reagan, "Inaugural Address, January 5, 1967."